IDEAS from the

ARITHMETIC TEACHER

Grades 6–8 Middle School

compiled by

George Immerzeel

Melvin Thomas

from original IDEAS prepared by

George Bright

Marilyn Burns

Joan Duea

George Immerzeel

Earl Ockenga

Don Wiederanders

Donald W. Scheuer, Jr.

David E. Williams

M. Bernadine Tabler

Marilyn Hall Jacobson

Copyright © 1982 by

The National Council of Teachers of Mathematics, Inc.
1906 Association Drive, Reston, Virginia 22091

Fourth printing 1990
Printed in the United States of America
ISBN 0-87353-200-7

Introduction

The IDEAS section has been a feature of the *Arithmetic Teacher* since 1971. This collection has been selected from those activities appropriate for students in grades 6 through 8. The selections have been reprinted just as they originally appeared in the journal.

On one side of each page you will find the Student Activity Sheet; the teacher directions are on the reverse. This booklet has been perforated so that the pages can be easily removed and reproduced for classroom use. We suggest that you make a file of these pages or punch them for storage in a loose-leaf binder. Copies should be kept in the same file or binder so that you can use them when they are needed.

This volume has been topically arranged so that IDEAS for computational skills, for example, appear in one section, IDEAS for problem solving are grouped in another section, and so on.

Table of Contents

Use these rules for each round.

Roll a die eight times.

After each roll, write the number shown on the die in one of the boxes. After a number is written in a box, it cannot be changed.

Find the two sums.

If the number sentence about the sums is correct and
  (a) both sums are three-digit numbers, score 10 points;
  (b) both sums are two-digit numbers, score 8 points;
  (c) only the larger sum is a three-digit number, score 4 points.

Otherwise, score 0 points.

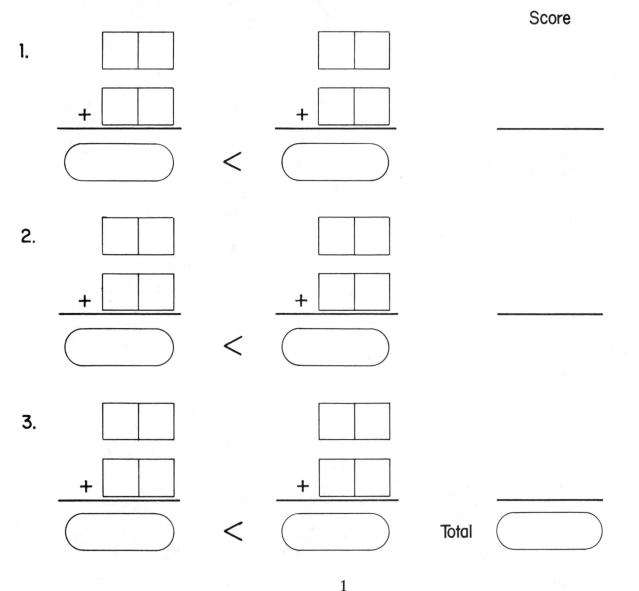

 For Teachers

Objective: To reinforce concepts of ordering and place value for
two-digit and three-digit
numbers

Going further:
1. Use a die labeled with the numbers 4
   through 9.
2. Use a die labeled only with even (or
   odd) numbers.
3. Use a die labeled as follows: 1, 2, 3,
   7, 8, 9.

Use these rules for each round.

Roll a die six times.

After each roll, write the number shown on the die in one of the boxes. After a number is written in a box, it cannot be changed.

If all three numbers are in order, score 10 points.
If only the first two numbers are in order, score 4 points.
If only the last two numbers are in order, score 4 points.

Otherwise, score 0 points.

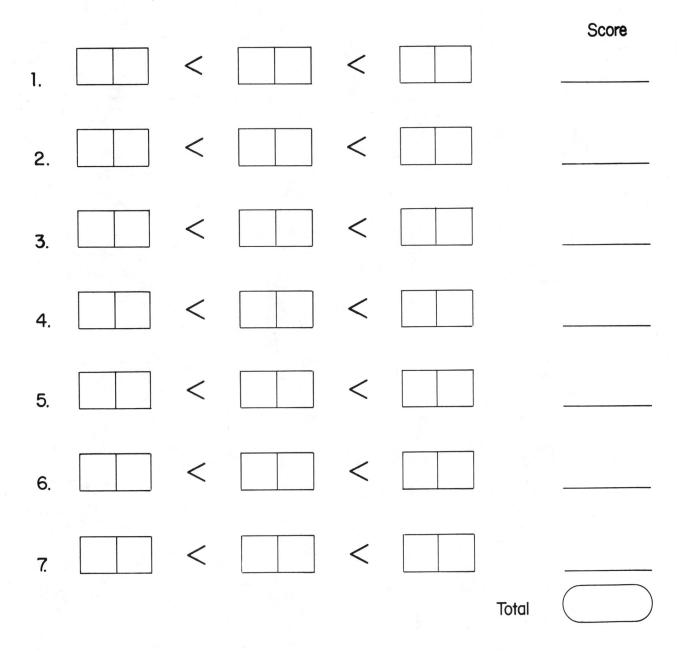

 **IDEAS** For Teachers

Objective: To reinforce concepts of ordering three, two-digit
numbers

Going Further:
1. Use a die labeled with the numbers 4
through 9.
2. Use a die labeled as follows: 7, 8, 8,
9, 9, 9.
3. Use a die labeled as follows: 3, 4, 4,
4, 4, 4.

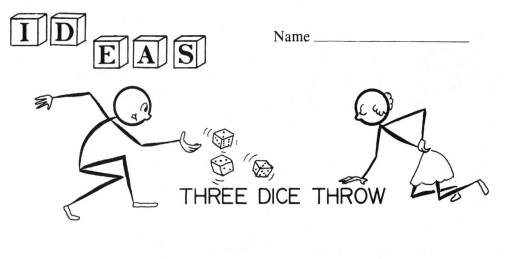

THREE DICE THROW

0	1	2	3	4	5	6	7
8	9	10	11	12	13	14	15
16	17	18	19	20	21	22	23
24	25	26	27	28	29	30	31
32	33	34	35	36	37	38	39

For two or three players. Players take turns.

1. Roll three dice.
2. Using any combination of operations (+, −, ×, ÷), make a number on the chart.
3. Cover the number that you make.
4. A number can be covered only once. If a player cannot make an uncovered number, play moves to the next player.

Scoring:

For each number covered, 1 point. If the box of the marked number touches any box with a marked already on it, an additional point is scored for each box touched.

For Teachers

Objective: Reinforcement in whole number operations.

Directions for teachers:

This is a game for two or three students. For each game, one copy of the activity sheet, THREE DICE THROW, is needed, along with three dice with 1, 2, 3, 4, 5, and 6 on each die. The rules for play are as follows:

1. Each player throws the three dice, then uses the three numbers to make any number on the playing board. Any operation or combination of operations may be used.

2. When a player makes a number, a marker is placed on that number on the playing board and the player scores 1 point.

3. If the box of the marked number touches any box with a marker already on it, an additional point is scored for each box touched.

0	1	2	3	4	5	6	7
8	9	10	11	12	13	14	15
16	17	18	19	20	21	22	23
24	25	26	27	28	29	30	31
32	33	34	35	36	37	38	39

Example: A play on 22 would score 1 for the play, plus 2 additional points for touching 14 and 2.

4. Players take turns throwing the dice. Play continues until the playing board is covered. The player with the highest score wins.

Going further:

1. Add a "challenge" rule. If a player feels that another player did not make the move that scored the most possible points, a challenge may be made. The player does not change the move, but the challenger gets the additional points the better move would have earned.

2. Enlarge the board for a longer game.

3. Use four dice instead of three.

IDEAS

1	2	3	4	5	6	7	8	9	10	11	12
2	4	6	8	10	12	14	16	18	20	22	24
3	6	9	12	15	18	21	24	27	30	33	36
4	8	12	16	20	24	28	32	36	40	44	48
5	10	15	20	25	30	35	40	45	50	55	60
6	12	18	24	30	36	42	48	54	60	66	72
7	14	21	28	35	42	49	56	63	70	77	84
8	16	24	32	40	48	56	64	72	80	88	96
9	18	27	36	45	54	63	72	81	90	99	108
10	20	30	40	50	60	70	80	90	100	110	120
11	22	33	44	55	66	77	88	99	110	121	132
12	24	36	48	60	72	84	96	108	120	132	144

 For Teachers

Objective: To give practice with multiples and the multiplication chart

Directions for teachers:

1. Duplicate a worksheet for each student.
2. Any number from 2 to 12 may go in the box. The student copies the multiples of that number from the chart and then continues the multiples down to a multiple closest to but no greater than 144.
3. Then the student colors every number on the list wherever it appears on the chart. It helps to have children cross the numbers off the list as they color the chart.
4. The charts should be posted and the patterns for the different numbers compared.

Going further:

If children wish to make their own complete "Multiplication Chart Pattern Books," they need to do 11 sheets, one for each of the numbers from 2 to 12. It is an ambitious project, but may interest some students.

Sample:

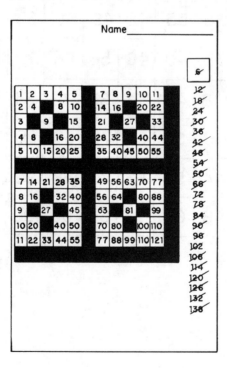

Multiplication Game (2 teams)

How to play:
1. Teams take turns. Pick any two of these numbers.

2. Multiply the numbers you picked.

3. Find the answer on the game board. Place your team's mark on it (X or O).

Game Board

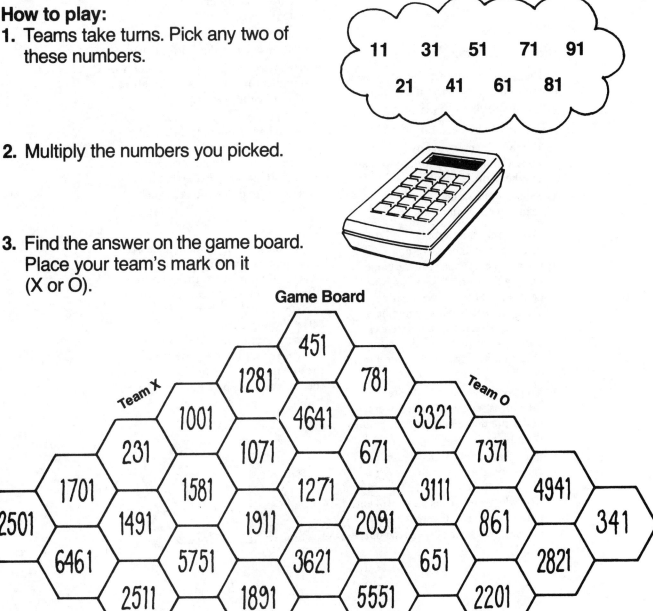

How to win: The first team to get a path of answers connecting its two sides of the game board wins.

☐☐☐☐☐☐ For Teachers

Objective: Experience in estimating
products

Directions for teachers:

The way you use the activities will
depend on the number of calculators
available to you.

If you have one calculator:

1. Remove the master copy and reproduce a transparency for use with an
   overhead projector.

2. Separate the students into two
   teams (team *X* and team *O*).

3. Project the transparency. Tell students there will be a five-minute
   warm-up before playing the game.
   During the warm-up session, students are to use their estimating
   skills to identify pairs of numbers
   whose answers (sums, differences,
   products, or quotients, depending
   on the game) are found on the game
   board.

4. To play the game, have the teams
   take turns selecting two numbers
   and using the calculator to compute
   the answer.

5. Each team finds its answer on the
   game board and puts the team's
   mark on it (*X* or *O*). The game is
   won when a team has an unbroken
   path of marked answers that connects its two sides of the game board
   (fig. 1).

If you have more than one calculator:

1. Remove the master copy and reproduce the worksheet.

2. Separate the students into teams,
   with two teams sharing a calculator.

3. Have teams take turns selecting two
   numbers and using the calculator to
   compute the answer.

4. Each team finds its answer on the
   game board and puts the team's
   mark on it (*X* or *O*). The game is
   won when a team has an unbroken
   path of marked answers that connects its two sides on the game
   board.

Comments:

Play the game more than once. At
first students may pick pairs of numbers at random, but as they play more
often they will start to develop strategies for using their estimation skills to
select the numbers.

An interesting modification of the
game is to require one player to pick
the first number and another player on
the same team to pick the second number.

Fig. 1

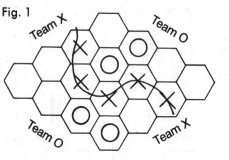

X _____

O _____

PINPOINTING PRODUCTS

RULES: Take turns.

1. Place the arrows on two of the numbers at the right.

2. Multiply these numbers.

3. Mark the answer on the game board with your mark, *X* or *O*.

The winner is the first player to get four marks in a line.

$$1 \quad 2 \quad 3$$
$$4 \quad 5 \quad 6$$
$$7 \quad 8 \quad 9$$

GAME BOARD

9	24	6	10	16	5
12	45	32	54	30	14
2	28	40	72	48	18
7	36	63	42	56	3
21	4	15	27	8	35

Objective: Experiences with multiplication, focusing on factors needed to get a desired product

Directions for teachers:
1. Remove the student activity sheet and make a transparency and at least one copy for each pair of students.
2. Using the transparency, play the game (teacher vs. students) so the students learn the rules.

Directions for pairs of students:
1. Cut out the arrows at the bottom of the page.

2. Sign your name by *X* or *O* at the top of the page.
3. Read the rules before playing the game.

Comments:
As students become effective players using the original rules, you may wish to make the game more challenging by allowing a player to move only one arrow on each turn. This way two numbers are identified by the arrows, but only one of the numbers is selected by the player. For example, if the arrows are on "4" and "6," the next player could move the arrow on "6" to the "8," giving the answer 32 (i.e., $4 \times 8 = 32$).

MENTAL MANEUVERS

X _____

O _____

RULES: Take turns.

1. Place the arrows on three of the numbers at the right.

2. Add two of the numbers and multiply the sum by the third number.

3. Mark the answer on the game board with your mark, *X* or *O*.

The winner is the first one to get four marks in a line.

1 2 3
4 5 6

GAME BOARD

32	5	24	15	22	14
48	18	40	12	44	28
9	11	42	27	33	10
30	16	50	20	35	21
54	36	8	25	45	7

Objective: Experiences with addition and multiplication, focusing on numbers and operations to get a desired an-

Directions for teachers:

1. **Remove the student activity sheet and make a transparency and at least one copy for each pair of students.**

2. **Using the transparency, play the game (teacher vs. students) so the students learn the rules.**

Directions for pairs of students:

1. Cut out the arrows at the bottom of the page.

2. Sign your name by *X* or *O* at the top of the page.

3. Read the rules before playing the game.

Comments:

A more challenging version of this game is to modify the rules so only one arrow may be moved. This way, three numbers identified by the arrows are used, but only one of them is chosen by the player. For example, if the arrows are on "1," "2," and "5," the arrow on "1" may be moved to "4." The answer then could be 30, from $(4 + 2) \times 5$; 28, from $(2 + 5) \times 4$; 18, from $(4 + 5) \times 2$; and so on.

License Plate Mathematics

Directions. Using the *last* digit in each plate as a target number, use the other digits, in any order, with the basic signs of operation to name the target number. (It may not be possible in every case.)

Example:

| 3A4723 | $[(7 - (4 + 2)] \times 3 = 3$ |

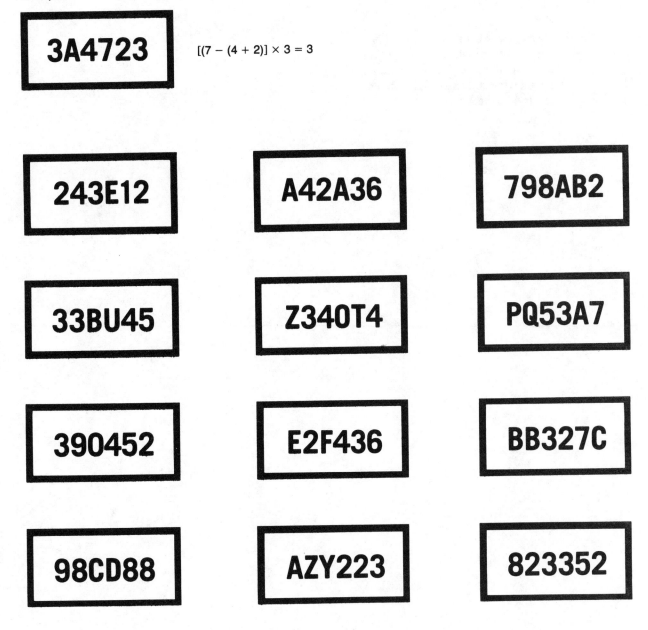

| 243E12 | A42A36 | 798AB2 |

| 33BU45 | Z340T4 | PQ53A7 |

| 390452 | E2F436 | BB327C |

| 98CD88 | AZY223 | 823352 |

⬛ **IDEAS** For Teachers

Objective: Experience in constructing number sentences using grouping and order of operations.

Directions for teachers:

1. Use master sheet to prepare a duplicating master for individual worksheets.

2. Have students follow directions on the worksheets and record their answers.

3. Discuss answers and possible alternative answers when necessary. You can individualize your instruction by allowing students to try different levels of the activity.

Name_____

Lead-Free Math

(No pencils allowed)

55 =

6 + 97	15 × 25
100 ÷ 25	184 − 129

106 =

636 ÷ 6	$\begin{array}{r} 79 \\ + 87 \end{array}$
$\begin{array}{r} 136 \\ - 68 \end{array}$	$\begin{array}{r} 26 \\ \times 6 \end{array}$

585 =

$\begin{array}{r} 834 \\ - 429 \end{array}$	$\begin{array}{r} 195 \\ \times 3 \end{array}$
19$\overline{)1235}$	$\begin{array}{r} 439 \\ + 316 \end{array}$

472 =

$\begin{array}{r} 75 \\ 233 \\ + 115 \end{array}$	$\begin{array}{r} 1289 \\ - 817 \end{array}$
$\begin{array}{r} 174 \\ \times 3 \end{array}$	1860 ÷ 5

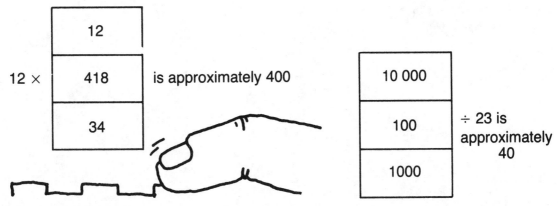

12 × $\begin{array}{|c|} \hline 12 \\ \hline 418 \\ \hline 34 \\ \hline \end{array}$ is approximately 400

$\begin{array}{|c|} \hline 10\ 000 \\ \hline 100 \\ \hline 1000 \\ \hline \end{array}$ ÷ 23 is approximately 40

Use a calculator to check your answers.

IDEAS

For Teachers

LEAD-FREE MATH

Objective

Practice in rounding off numbers and in estimating the results of addition, subtraction, multiplication, and division with whole numbers.

Materials needed

• Six markers (chips, cubes, pieces of paper, beans, paper clips, or anything else that will fit in the squares on the worksheet) per student.
• Calculators

Review

How to round off numbers and make estimates

Directions for teachers

1. Without writing anything down, students should estimate the answer to each example in the squares and put a marker in the square that would give an answer closest to the answer given.

2. For the last two problems, students should put a marker on the number that will give the indicated answers.

3. When they are finished, the students should check their answers with a calculator.

Answers

$184 - 129$; $636 \div 6$; 195×3; $1289 - 817$; 34; 1000

Name_____

Calendar Computation

November

Sunday	Monday	Tuesday	Wednesday	Thursday	Friday	Saturday
						1
2	3	4	5	6	7	8
9	10	11	12	13	14	15
16	17	18	19	20	21	22
23	24	25	26	27	28	29
30						

Number Pattern

1. Draw a ring around the multiples of 7. Do you see a pattern?
2. Would you see a pattern for the multiples of 7 in December?   □ Yes   □ No
   Why or why not?

DECEMBER
S M T W T F S
      1 2 3 4 5 6
7 8 9 10 11 12 13
14 15 16 17 18 19 20
21 22 23 24 25 26 27
28 29 30 31

Column Addition

3. Add the dates of all Mondays for this month. _____
4. Add the dates of all Tuesdays for this month. _____
5. Add the dates of all Wednesdays for this month. _____
6. Look at your answers. What pattern do you notice?_____
7. Use the pattern to guess what the sum of all Thursdays will be. _____ guess.
8. Add to check your guess. Were you correct?   □ Yes   □ No

Average

9. Find the average of the numbers located inside the box marked on the calendar. _____
10. Mark off another 3-by-3 set of numbers on the calendar. Find the average of those numbers. _____
11. Look at the two averages. What pattern do you notice? _____
12. What will be the average for any 3-by-3 set of numbers? _____

For Teachers

CALENDAR COMPUTATION

Objective

To provide computational practice and to develop an awareness of number patterns on the calendar.

Materials needed

Worksheet, possibly a calendar for the year.

Directions

Encourage students to look for the patterns in the three parts of the worksheet. Following the completion of the worksheet, have them verbalize the patterns they have noticed.

Extensions

Explore patterns for multiples of 6 and 8.

Column addition: Ask students to see if the pattern continues for Thursday, Friday, and Saturday. Have them explain their answer.

Answers

(1) Multiples of 7 are in a straight row. (2) Yes, because the calendar is based on 7 days a week. Therefore the multiples of 7 will always be in a straight row. (3) 54. (4) 58. (5) 62. (6) The sums are 4 more each time. (8) 66. (9) 10. (11) The average is the middle number. (12) Middle number.

Name_____

Use a ruler to draw a line segment between each pair of fractions whose sum is 1.

Count all the squares

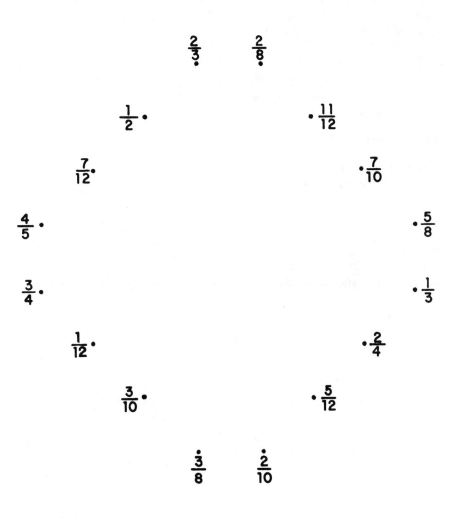

Objective: To practice adding fractions whose sum is 1

Directions for teachers:

1. Give each student a copy of the worksheet.

2. Let the students read the directions. Emphasize that the students are looking for pairs of fractions whose sum is 1; for example, $\frac{3}{8} + \frac{5}{8}$ or $\frac{2}{3} + \frac{1}{3}$. The use of straightedges will make the drawings more accurate, but you do not need to insist on their use.

3. Three fractions, $\frac{2}{8}$, $\frac{2}{4}$, and $\frac{2}{10}$, are not in lowest terms. If students have trouble matching these fractions with

$$\frac{3}{4}, \frac{1}{2}, \text{ and } \frac{4}{5},$$

respectively, suggest to the students that they rewrite all fractions in lowest terms before trying to match them.

4. After the students have drawn all the line segments, encourage them to identify not only the simplest squares; for example, ◇ ; but also more complex ones.

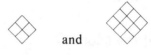

The total number of squares is 14.

Answer:

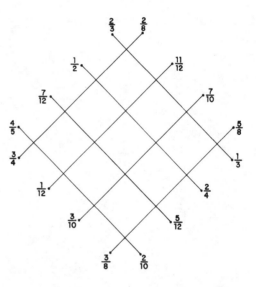

Follow the arrows.

A.

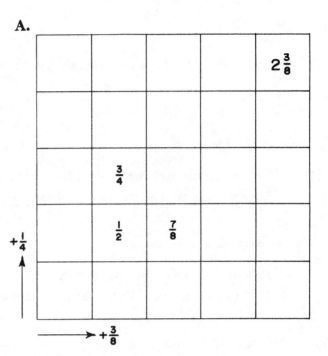

B.

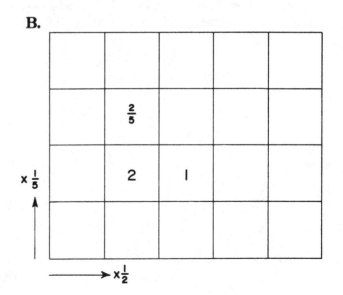

For Teachers

Objective: Computational practice with addition and multiplication of fractions.

Directions for teachers:

1. Tear out student worksheet and reproduce one copy for each student.
2. Draw a similar table on the blackboard and complete the table in class.

Directions to be read to students:

1. Follow the arrows to complete the table.
2. Look for patterns that will help you check your work.

Comments: Tables like these are easily made up and give computational practice that is fun. You may also wish to explain the meaning for other arrows such as ↗, ↘, or ↙, or make combinations of arrows and interpret these arrows and their combinations in terms of fraction operations.

Name _____

Study the example and complete each move.

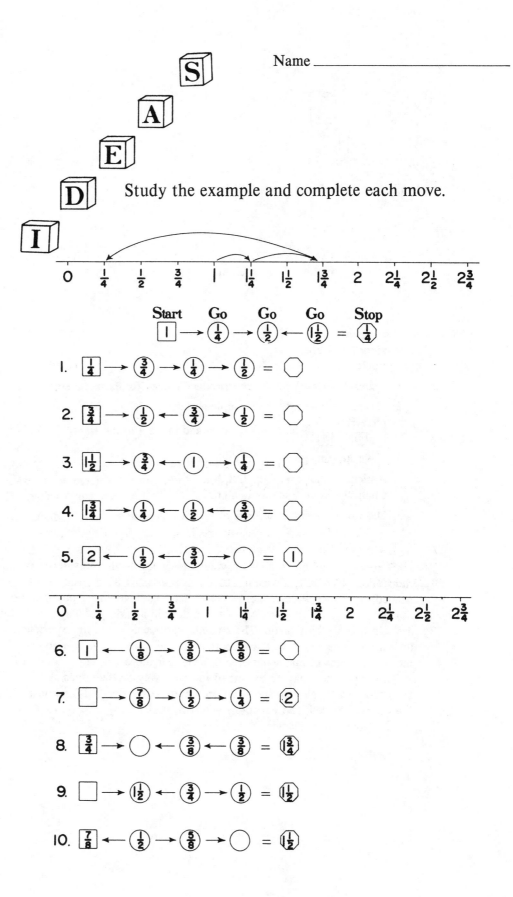

0   $\frac{1}{4}$ $\frac{1}{2}$ $\frac{3}{4}$ 1 $1\frac{1}{4}$ $1\frac{1}{2}$ $1\frac{3}{4}$ 2 $2\frac{1}{4}$ $2\frac{1}{2}$ $2\frac{3}{4}$

Start **Go** **Go** **Go** **Stop**

$\boxed{1} \rightarrow \left(\frac{1}{4}\right) \rightarrow \left(\frac{1}{2}\right) \leftarrow \left(1\frac{1}{2}\right) = \left(\frac{1}{4}\right)$

1. $\boxed{\frac{1}{4}} \rightarrow \left(\frac{3}{4}\right) \rightarrow \left(\frac{1}{4}\right) \rightarrow \left(\frac{1}{2}\right) = \bigcirc$

2. $\boxed{\frac{3}{4}} \rightarrow \left(\frac{1}{2}\right) \leftarrow \left(\frac{3}{4}\right) \rightarrow \left(\frac{1}{2}\right) = \bigcirc$

3. $\boxed{1\frac{1}{2}} \rightarrow \left(\frac{3}{4}\right) \leftarrow \left(1\right) \rightarrow \left(\frac{1}{4}\right) = \bigcirc$

4. $\boxed{1\frac{3}{4}} \rightarrow \left(\frac{1}{4}\right) \leftarrow \left(\frac{1}{2}\right) \leftarrow \left(\frac{3}{4}\right) = \bigcirc$

5. $\boxed{2} \leftarrow \left(\frac{1}{2}\right) \leftarrow \left(\frac{3}{4}\right) \rightarrow \bigcirc = \left(1\right)$

0   $\frac{1}{4}$ $\frac{1}{2}$ $\frac{3}{4}$ 1 $1\frac{1}{4}$ $1\frac{1}{2}$ $1\frac{3}{4}$ 2 $2\frac{1}{4}$ $2\frac{1}{2}$ $2\frac{3}{4}$

6. $\boxed{1} \leftarrow \left(\frac{1}{8}\right) \rightarrow \left(\frac{3}{8}\right) \rightarrow \left(\frac{5}{8}\right) = \bigcirc$

7. $\boxed{} \rightarrow \left(\frac{7}{8}\right) \rightarrow \left(\frac{1}{2}\right) \rightarrow \left(\frac{1}{4}\right) = \left(2\right)$

8. $\boxed{\frac{3}{4}} \rightarrow \bigcirc \leftarrow \left(\frac{3}{8}\right) \leftarrow \left(\frac{3}{8}\right) = \left(1\frac{3}{4}\right)$

9. $\boxed{} \rightarrow \left(1\frac{1}{2}\right) \leftarrow \left(\frac{3}{4}\right) \rightarrow \left(\frac{1}{2}\right) = \left(1\frac{1}{2}\right)$

10. $\boxed{\frac{7}{8}} \leftarrow \left(\frac{1}{2}\right) \rightarrow \left(\frac{5}{8}\right) \rightarrow \bigcirc = \left(1\frac{1}{2}\right)$

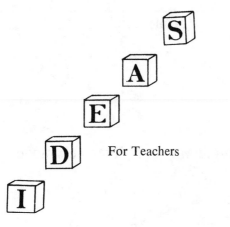

For Teachers

Objective: Number line experience with fractions

Directions for teachers:

1. Remove the worksheet and reproduce a copy for each student.

2. Have students study the example and discuss it.
   $\left(\dfrac{\text{START GO}}{\boxed{m} \rightarrow \boxed{n}} \text{ is read: "Start at } m \text{ and move } n \text{ to the right."}\right)$

3. Have students go ahead on their own.

4. Anticipate that exercises 7, 8, and 9 will cause considerable frustration. Challenge your students to figure out solutions they can "defend."

5. Discuss the various methods of solution devised by your students.

Comments: These exercises provide experiences with equivalence of fractions (i.e., ½ = ⁴⁄₈), inverses (i.e., →(½)←(½) = 0) as well as the much needed experience with fractions greater than one involving a physical model. Students will approach exercises of this nature in a variety of ways unless they are told how to think or do. The student who needs counting experiences on the number line will have that experience. The student who has good insight into the patterns of mathematics will devise far more efficient procedures.

This experience may be expanded in many ways: Other special subsets of fractions may be chosen, such as thirds and sixths; decimal-fraction number lines could be used; and equations with two variables ((¼)→ ○ ← ○ →(½) = (1)) would be challenging.

Answers

1. $1\frac{3}{4}$ 3. $1\frac{1}{2}$ 5. $\frac{1}{4}$ 7. $\frac{3}{8}$ 9. $\frac{1}{4}$

2. 1 4. $\frac{3}{4}$ 6. $1\frac{7}{8}$ 8. $1\frac{3}{4}$ 10. $\frac{1}{2}$

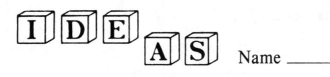

Name _____

Directions: Cut out the squares. Fit them together so that the edges that touch name the same number.

A 4 × 4 grid of squares, each square labeled with fractions/decimals on its edges (top, left, right, bottom):

Row 1
- Square 1: top $\frac{2}{4}$, left 1, right $\frac{4}{12}$, bottom $\frac{1}{7}$
- Square 2: top 2, left $\frac{2}{10}$, right $\frac{1}{8}$, bottom $\frac{3}{2}$
- Square 3: top $\frac{7}{10}$, right $\frac{3}{7}$
- Square 4: right $\frac{2}{3}$, bottom $\frac{1}{4}$

Row 2
- Square 1: left $\frac{2}{12}$, bottom $\frac{3}{5}$
- Square 2: top $\frac{5}{3}$, left $\frac{8}{10}$, right $\frac{3}{3}$, bottom $\frac{6}{3}$
- Square 3: top $\frac{2}{14}$, left $\frac{2}{16}$, right $\frac{5}{8}$, bottom $\frac{3}{4}$
- Square 4: top $\frac{1}{3}$, left $\frac{1}{2}$

Row 3
- Square 1: top $\frac{6}{16}$, left $\frac{10}{16}$, bottom $\frac{2}{6}$
- Square 2: top $\frac{6}{8}$, left $\frac{3}{10}$, right $\frac{12}{24}$
- Square 3: top $\frac{10}{12}$, right $\frac{1}{5}$, bottom $.7$
- Square 4: top $1\frac{1}{2}$, left $\frac{6}{14}$, right $.3$

Row 4
- Square 1: left $\frac{4}{6}$, right $\frac{0}{2}$, bottom $1\frac{2}{3}$
- Square 2: top $\frac{2}{8}$, right $\frac{4}{5}$, bottom $\frac{5}{6}$
- Square 3: left 0, right $\frac{1}{6}$, bottom $\frac{1}{2}$
- Square 4: top $\frac{6}{10}$, left $\frac{1}{3}$, bottom $\frac{3}{8}$

Objective: Experience with the concept of equals.

Directions:

1. Provide each student with a copy of the activity sheet and a pair of scissors.

2. If necessary, give the hint that when the squares are fit together correctly, a 4 by 4 square is once again found.

Comments: The fewer directions required the better. Students need experience in figuring things out for themselves.

Name_____

Put the letters on the right box.

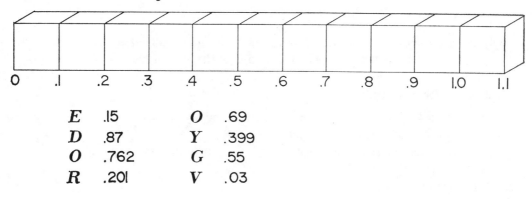

E	.15	O	.69
D	.87	Y	.399
O	.762	G	.55
R	.201	V	.03

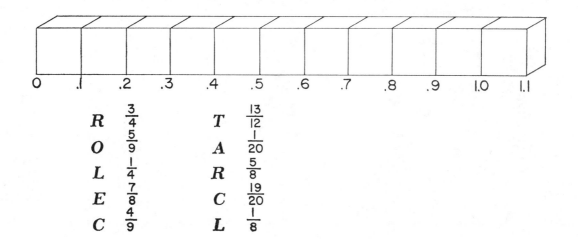

R	$\frac{3}{4}$	T	$\frac{13}{12}$
O	$\frac{5}{9}$	A	$\frac{1}{20}$
L	$\frac{1}{4}$	R	$\frac{5}{8}$
E	$\frac{7}{8}$	C	$\frac{19}{20}$
C	$\frac{4}{9}$	L	$\frac{1}{8}$

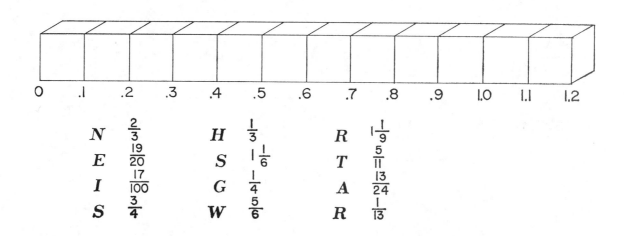

N	$\frac{2}{3}$	H	$\frac{1}{3}$	R	$1\frac{1}{9}$
E	$\frac{19}{20}$	S	$1\frac{1}{6}$	T	$\frac{5}{11}$
I	$\frac{17}{100}$	G	$1\frac{1}{4}$	A	$\frac{13}{24}$
S	$\frac{3}{4}$	W	$\frac{5}{6}$	R	$\frac{1}{13}$

IDEAS for Fractions and Decimals   29

Objective: Experiences in ordering numbers that encourage estimation rather than computation using a modification of the number line

Directions for teachers:

1. Give each student a copy of the appropriate activity sheet.
2. Have them read the directions and go to work.
3. Observe each student individually to be sure that the directions are carried out.

Comments: After most of the students have completed naming the *second row* of boxes, you may wish to encourage estimating by commenting: "Some students seem to be able to figure out which box a letter goes on by estimating rather than doing the computation."

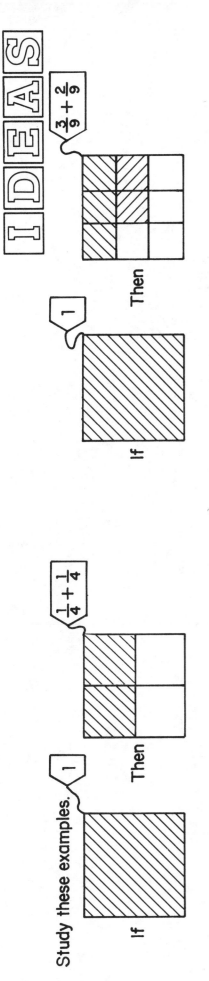

IDEAS

Study these examples.

If ⌐1⌐ Then

If ⌐1⌐ Then $\frac{1}{4} + \frac{1}{4}$

If ⌐1⌐ Then $\frac{3}{9} + \frac{2}{9}$

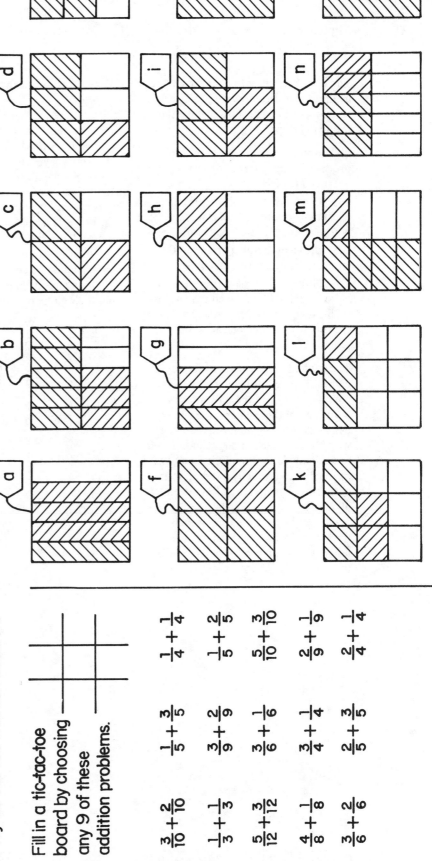

Play tic-tac-toe fraction addition.

Fill in a tic-tac-toe board by choosing any 9 of these addition problems.

$\frac{3}{10} + \frac{2}{10}$	$\frac{1}{5} + \frac{3}{5}$	$\frac{1}{4} + \frac{1}{4}$
$\frac{1}{3} + \frac{1}{3}$	$\frac{3}{9} + \frac{2}{9}$	$\frac{1}{5} + \frac{2}{5}$
$\frac{5}{12} + \frac{3}{12}$	$\frac{3}{6} + \frac{1}{6}$	$\frac{5}{10} + \frac{3}{10}$
$\frac{4}{8} + \frac{1}{8}$	$\frac{3}{4} + \frac{1}{4}$	$\frac{2}{9} + \frac{1}{9}$
$\frac{3}{6} + \frac{2}{6}$	$\frac{2}{5} + \frac{3}{5}$	$\frac{2}{4} + \frac{1}{4}$

 For Teachers

Objective: Experience in adding fractions

The IDEA this month is to use an overhead projector to provide practice with fractions. For each activity, take the following steps:

1. Remove the master copy and reproduce a transparency for use with an overhead projector.

2. Cover up each of the fifteen lettered unit squares (pennies work well) before turning on the projector.

3. Project the transparency and have students study the two examples.

4. Have each student draw a tic-tac-toe board and fill in the empty spaces on his board by writing in any nine of the fractions shown on the transparency.

The students are now ready to play the games. Each game begins with the uncovering of one of the unit squares.

In each of these games, the winner can be determined in more than one way. The winner can be the first player to correctly letter three cells in a row, or the first to correctly letter all four corners, or the first to correctly letter all nine fractions.

Check players' thinking in each of the games by having them tell what letters they matched to each of the fractions.

Directions for teachers:

Play tic-tac-toe fraction addition with your students. As each of the lettered unit squares on the transparency is uncovered, players must decide what addition problem is described by the shaded parts of the unit square. If the corresponding addition problem is on the player's tic-tac-toe board, he writes the tag letter beside it.

You may expand the experience by having students choose any nine of the following addition problems in filling out their game boards.

$$\frac{1}{2}+\frac{1}{8} \qquad \frac{1}{2}+\frac{3}{10} \qquad \frac{3}{4}+\frac{1}{4}$$

$$\frac{1}{5}+\frac{2}{5} \qquad \frac{1}{2}+\frac{1}{4} \qquad \frac{5}{12}+\frac{1}{4}$$

$$\frac{1}{3}+\frac{1}{3} \qquad \frac{2}{9}+\frac{1}{9} \qquad \frac{1}{4}+\frac{1}{4}$$

$$\frac{1}{2}+\frac{1}{3} \qquad \frac{1}{5}+\frac{3}{5} \qquad \frac{1}{2}+\frac{1}{6}$$

$$\frac{1}{3}+\frac{2}{9} \qquad \frac{2}{5}+\frac{3}{5} \qquad \frac{3}{10}+\frac{1}{5}$$

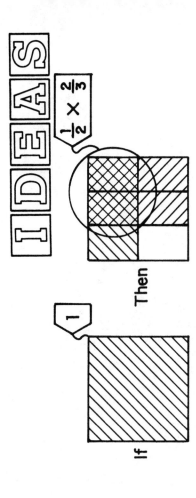

Study these examples.

If [1] Then

$\frac{1}{2} \times \frac{1}{2}$

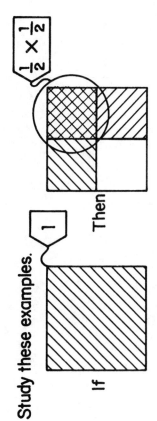

$\frac{1}{2} \times \frac{2}{3}$

IDEAS

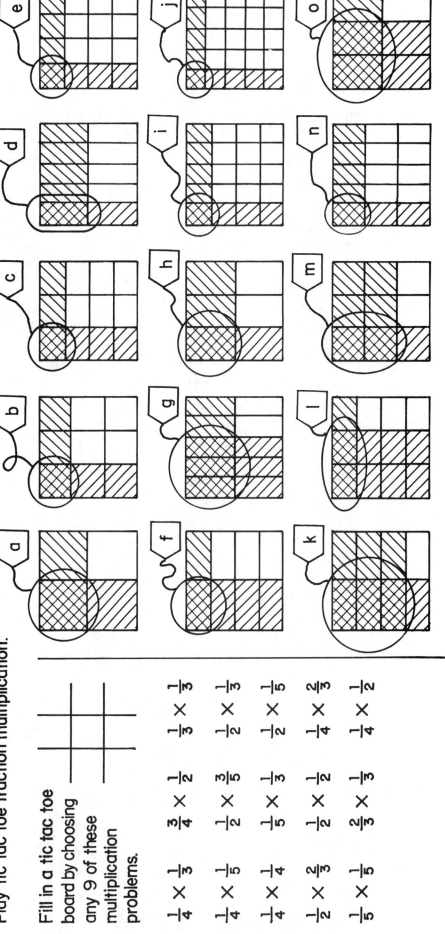

Play tic tac toe fraction multiplication.

Fill in a tic tac toe board by choosing any 9 of these multiplication problems.

$\frac{1}{4} \times \frac{1}{3}$ $\frac{3}{4} \times \frac{1}{2}$ $\frac{1}{3} \times \frac{1}{3}$

$\frac{1}{4} \times \frac{1}{5}$ $\frac{1}{2} \times \frac{3}{5}$ $\frac{1}{2} \times \frac{1}{3}$

$\frac{1}{4} \times \frac{1}{4}$ $\frac{1}{5} \times \frac{1}{3}$ $\frac{1}{2} \times \frac{1}{5}$

$\frac{1}{2} \times \frac{2}{3}$ $\frac{1}{2} \times \frac{1}{2}$ $\frac{1}{4} \times \frac{2}{3}$

$\frac{1}{5} \times \frac{1}{5}$ $\frac{2}{3} \times \frac{1}{3}$ $\frac{1}{4} \times \frac{1}{2}$

Objective: Experience with multiplication of fractions

Directions for teachers:

You may choose to use a chalkboard unit square to reinforce the students' understanding of the following example:

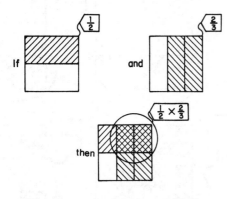

Play tic-tac-toe fraction multiplication with your students. The game starts when one of the lettered unit squares on the transparency is uncovered. Players must then decide what multiplication problem is described by

the double crosshatch shading (▨)

of that unit square. If the multiplication problem is on a player's tic-tac-toe board, he writes the tag letter beside it. Play continues as other lettered squares on the transparency are uncovered one at a time.

You could modify this experience by having students fill out their board with any nine of the following products.

$$\frac{1}{10} \quad \frac{1}{8} \quad \frac{1}{3} \quad \frac{2}{12} \quad \frac{1}{6}$$

$$\frac{2}{9} \quad \frac{1}{25} \quad \frac{1}{15} \quad \frac{3}{8} \quad \frac{1}{4}$$

$$\frac{1}{16} \quad \frac{1}{20} \quad \frac{1}{12} \quad \frac{2}{6} \quad \frac{3}{10}$$

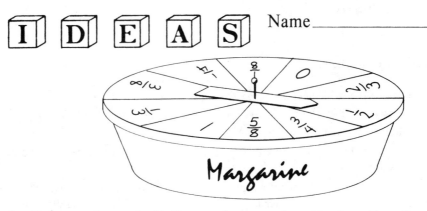

Name_____

1. Spin and mark (**✗**) a point on the number line for each outcome.

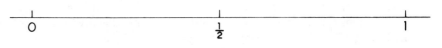

0   ½   1

2. Write the outcome in a ☐. The first player to complete 10 true statements is the winner.

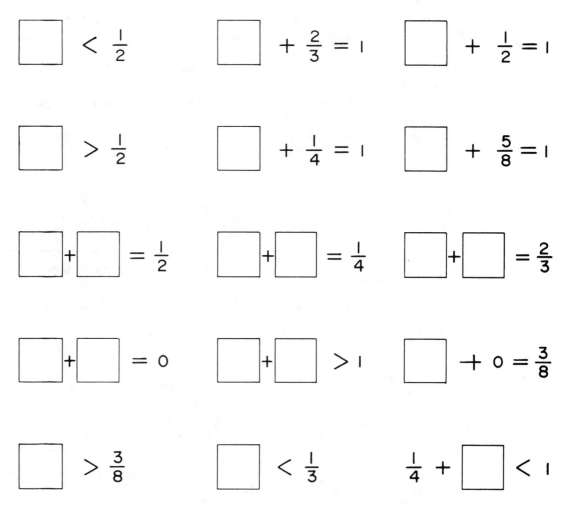

☐ < $\frac{1}{2}$ ☐ + $\frac{2}{3}$ = 1   ☐ + $\frac{1}{2}$ = 1

☐ > $\frac{1}{2}$ ☐ + $\frac{1}{4}$ = 1   ☐ + $\frac{5}{8}$ = 1

☐ + ☐ = $\frac{1}{2}$ ☐ + ☐ = $\frac{1}{4}$ ☐ + ☐ = $\frac{2}{3}$

☐ + ☐ = 0   ☐ + ☐ > 1   ☐ + 0 = $\frac{3}{8}$

☐ > $\frac{3}{8}$ ☐ < $\frac{1}{3}$ $\frac{1}{4}$ + ☐ < 1

IDEAS For Teachers

Objective: Experience with equations and inequalities

Directions for teachers:

1. Remove the worksheet and reproduce a copy for each student.
2. Construct one or more spinners for your class. (Directions follow.)
3. Allow the students to experiment with the spinner.
4. Encourage the students to study the sentences on their worksheet as you explain how the game is played.

The game is played in pairs. The outcome of each spin is announced. The players take turns entering the outcome of each spin in a □ to make a true sentence. The opponent is responsible for checking to make sure the player's sentence is true. The first player to correctly complete ten sentences wins the game.

Comments: Ideally, each pair of players should have their own spinner. Then the players take turns spinning and completing the sentence of their choice.

Variations can easily be made to adjust the level of difficulty for the needs of your students. Disks may be made with fewer or more possible outcomes. You may also choose a different set of sentences and enter appropriate numbers as possible outcomes.

Directions for making the spinners:

1. Collect a container with a plastic top for each spinner desired.
2. Remove this sheet and reproduce one copy of the disk(s) for each spinner.
3. Cut out the disks and arrows. (You may wish to reinforce the arrows by gluing them to tagboard.)
4. Write these numerals on the larger disk: "0," "1/8," "1/4," "3/8," "1/3," "1," "5/8," "3/4," "1/2," "2/3."
5. Assemble each spinner by pinning the disk on the plastic top, using a straight pin as a center post.
6. For a more difficult game, the numerals 0–9 are written on both disks, and both disks are pinned to the plastic top, the smaller disk on top.

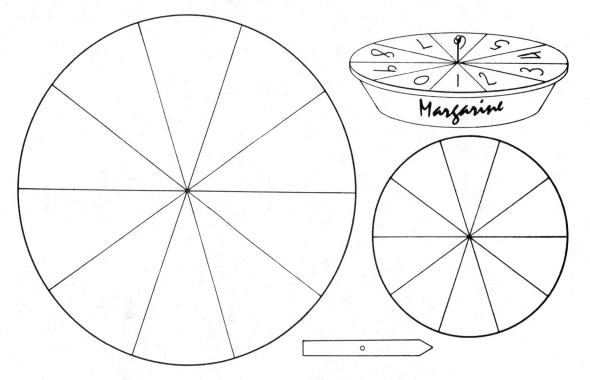

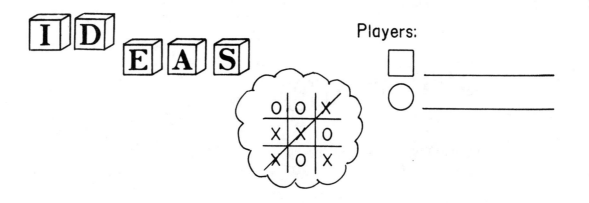

Players:

☐ _____

◯ _____

Rules:
1. Play by taking turns placing your mark (☐ or ◯) on a fraction.

2. Win **only** if you get three in a row <u>that</u> <u>are in order</u> (smallest to largest or largest to smallest).

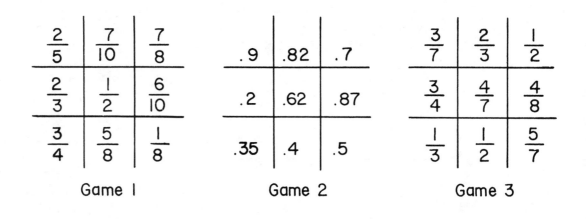

$\frac{2}{5}$	$\frac{7}{10}$	$\frac{7}{8}$
$\frac{2}{3}$	$\frac{1}{2}$	$\frac{6}{10}$
$\frac{3}{4}$	$\frac{5}{8}$	$\frac{1}{8}$

Game 1

.9	.82	.7
.2	.62	.87
.35	.4	.5

Game 2

$\frac{3}{7}$	$\frac{2}{3}$	$\frac{1}{2}$
$\frac{3}{4}$	$\frac{4}{7}$	$\frac{4}{8}$
$\frac{1}{3}$	$\frac{1}{2}$	$\frac{5}{7}$

Game 3

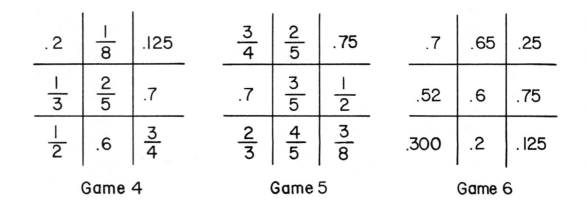

.2	$\frac{1}{8}$	.125
$\frac{1}{3}$	$\frac{2}{5}$	.7
$\frac{1}{2}$	.6	$\frac{3}{4}$

Game 4

$\frac{3}{4}$	$\frac{2}{5}$	.75
.7	$\frac{3}{5}$	$\frac{1}{2}$
$\frac{2}{3}$	$\frac{4}{5}$	$\frac{3}{8}$

Game 5

.7	.65	.25
.52	.6	.75
.300	.2	.125

Game 6

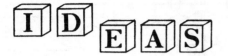 For Teachers

Objective: Experience with ordering fractions

Directions for teachers:

1. Remove the activity sheet and reproduce a copy for each student.
2. Have students read and discuss the directions. Be sure they understand that *two* criteria must be met to win.
3. After playing several games, have students discuss possible game strategies.
4. Have students try to make up game grids with as many potential ways to win as they can.

Comments: This take-off on tic-tac-toe forces the student to "read" the fraction symbols. You may wish to design more grids that have either common fractions only or decimal fractions only in them. Grids that are very easy or that are very hard may be constructed.

Division Game (2 teams)

How to play:
1. Teams take turns. Pick any two of these numbers.

2. Divide the numbers you picked

3. If the answer is on the game board, place your team's mark on it (X or O).

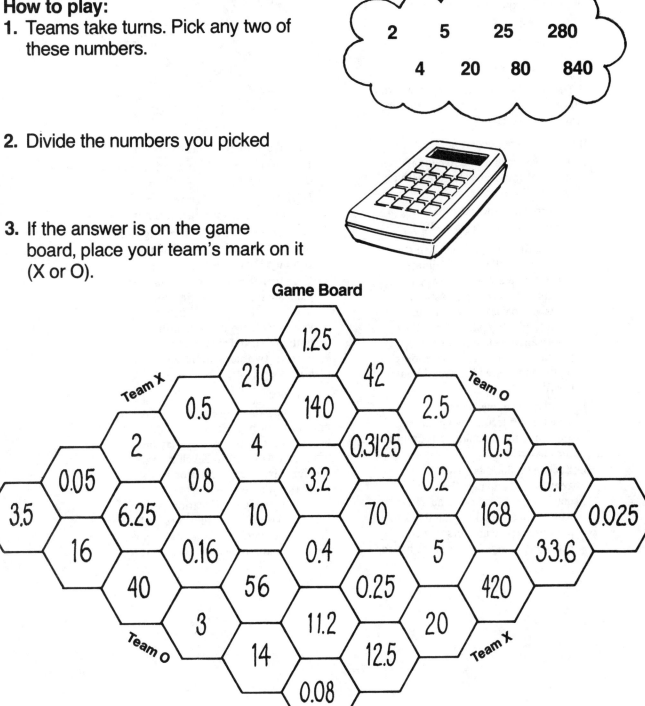

Game Board

How to win: The first team to get a path of answers connecting its two sides of the game board wins.

 For Teachers

Objective: Experience in estimating quotients

Directions for teachers:

The way you use the activities will depend on the number of calculators available to you.

If you have one calculator:

1. Remove the master copy and reproduce a transparency for use with an overhead projector.

2. Separate the students into two teams (team *X* and team *O*).

3. Project the transparency. Tell students there will be a five-minute warm-up before playing the game. During the warm-up session, students are to use their estimating skills to identify pairs of numbers whose answers (sums, differences, products, or quotients, depending on the game) are found on the game board.

4. To play the game, have the teams take turns selecting two numbers and using the calculator to compute the answer.

5. Each team finds its answer on the game board and puts the team's mark on it (*X* or *O*). The game is won when a team has an unbroken path of marked answers that connects its two sides of the game board (fig. 1).

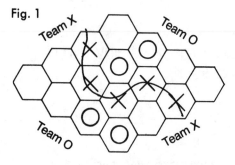
Fig. 1

If you have more than one calculator:

1. Remove the master copy and reproduce the worksheet.

2. Separate the students into teams, with two teams sharing a calculator.

3. Have teams take turns selecting two numbers and using the calculator to compute the answer.

4. Each team finds its answer on the game board and puts the team's mark on it (*X* or *O*). The game is won when a team has an unbroken path of marked answers that connects its two sides on the game board.

Comments:

Play the game more than once. At first students may pick pairs of numbers at random, but as they play more often they will start to develop strategies for using their estimation skills to select the numbers.

An interesting modification of the game is to require one player to pick the first number and another player on the same team to pick the second number.

Name _____

This is a magic square.   The magic sum is ____.

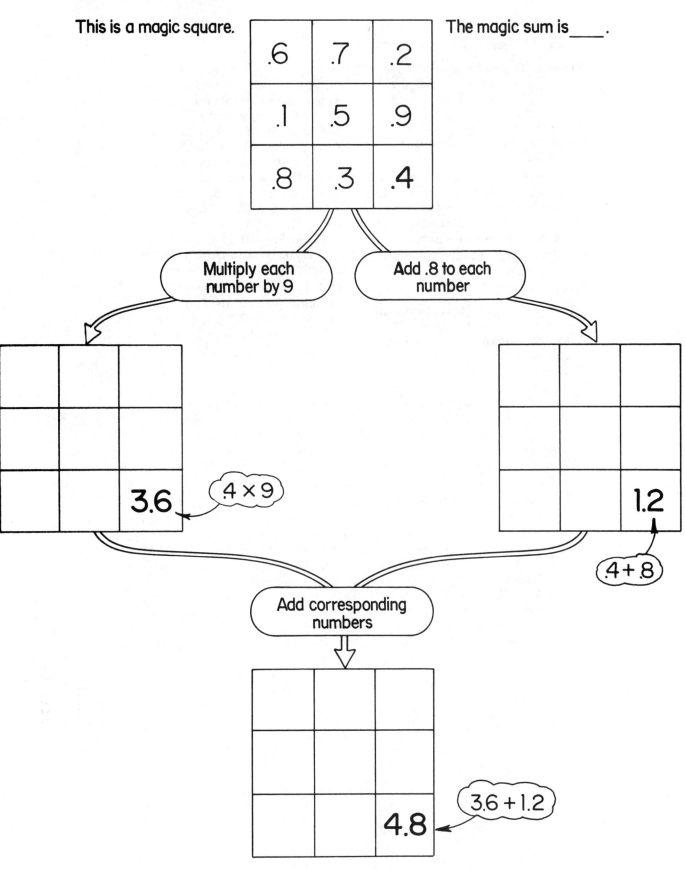

.6	.7	.2
.1	.5	.9
.8	.3	.4

Multiply each number by 9   **Add .8 to each number**

3.6   (.4 × 9)

1.2

(.4 + .8)

Add corresponding numbers

4.8   (3.6 + 1.2)

IDEAS For Teachers

Objective: To practice multiplication
and addition of decimals

Directions for teachers:

1. Give each student a copy of the
   worksheet.
2. Let the students read the directions
   and begin work. It is important that
   students understand that answers
   are to be written in the same rela-
   tive positions in each square.
3. Tell students to find the magic sum
   for each square.

Going further:

1. Help students see that each entry in
   the last square is .8 more than 10
   times the corresponding entry in the
   first square; for example, $4.8 = .4(10) + .8$. That is, in the last magic
   square, the whole number part of
   each entry is the same digit that appeared as the decimal part of the
   corresponding entry in the first
   magic square. The decimal part of
   each entry is .8, which is the amount
   added in the right-hand path. For
   example, $4.8 = 3.6 + 1.2 = .4(9) + (.4 + .8) = .4(9) + .4(1) + .8 = .4(10) + .8 = 4.0 + .8$. This result
   is based on the associative property
   of addition and distributive property of multiplication over addition.

2. The magic sums of the four magic
   squares are 1.5, $13.5 = 1.5(9)$, $3.9 = 1.5 + 3(.8)$, and $17.4 = 13.5 + 3.9$
   or $17.4 = 1.5(10) + 3(.8)$.

IDEAS

PLAY ESTIMATING DECIMAL SUMS

Pick two numbers.

Mark them with an X.

32.6	2.8	29.6	19.11	41.72	23.7	40.3	32.5	10.8
7.48	5.71	45.2	29.5	0.82	0.86	3.26	19.9	0.93
3.66	13.6	38.1	47.3	5.91	7.18			

Add the numbers you picked.

Find the box for your answer.

Keep track of your points.

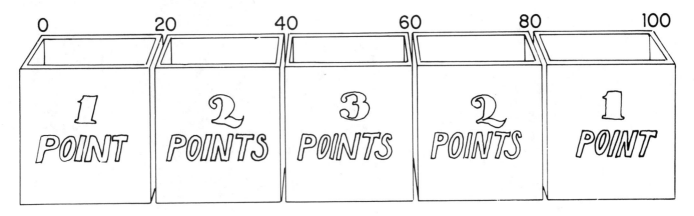

 For Teachers

Objective: Experience in estimating
decimal sums

Directions for teachers:

The way you use the activities will depend on the number of calculators available to you.

If you have one calculator:

1. Remove the master copy and reproduce a transparency for use with an overhead projector.

2. Project the transparency. Have students take turns selecting two numbers and using the calculator to find the answer.

3. Determine in which box the answer belongs and score the number of points listed on that box. The game is finished when all numbers have been selected once.

4. Play several games trying to improve the total class score each time.

If you have more than one calculator:

1. Remove the master copy and reproduce the worksheet.

2. Separate the students into teams with two teams sharing a calculator.

3. Have teams take turns selecting two numbers and using the calculator to find the answer.

4. Determine in which box the answer belongs and score the number of points listed on that box. The game is finished when all numbers have been selected once.

All the estimating activities may be modified for your students by changing the numbers at the top of each page or by changing the points for scoring the game at the bottom of each page.

After the students understand how to play the game, worksheets and a calculator could be placed in a learning center. The learning center provides the opportunity for students to work alone or in small teams to play the game.

Name_____

PLAY ESTIMATING DECIMAL PRODUCTS

Pick two numbers.

Mark them with an X.

3.6	0.03	13.1	29.6	11.9	0.7	33.7
0.04	21.9	.125	10.1	0.42	0.07	2.9
0.92	19.5	5.52	23.1	9.6	1.8	

Multiply the numbers you picked.

Find the box for your answer.

Keep track of your points.

 For Teachers

Objective: Experience in estimating decimal products

Directions for teachers:

The way you use the activities will depend on the number of calculators available to you.

If you have one calculator:

1. Remove the master copy and reproduce a transparency for use with an overhead projector.

2. Project the transparency. Have students take turns selecting two numbers and using the calculator to find the answer.

3. Determine in which box the answer belongs and score the number of points listed on that box. The game is finished when all numbers have been selected once.

4. Play several games trying to improve the total class score each time.

If you have more than one calculator:

1. Remove the master copy and reproduce the worksheet.

2. Separate the students into teams with two teams sharing a calculator.

3. Have teams take turns selecting two numbers and using the calculator to find the answer.

4. Determine in which box the answer belongs and score the number of points listed on that box. The game is finished when all numbers have been selected once.

All the estimating activities may be modified for your students by changing the numbers at the top of each page or by changing the points for scoring the game at the bottom of each page.

After the students understand how to play the game, worksheets and a calculator could be placed in a learning center. The learning center provides the opportunity for students to work alone or in small teams to play the game.

More (Pyramid) Power to You

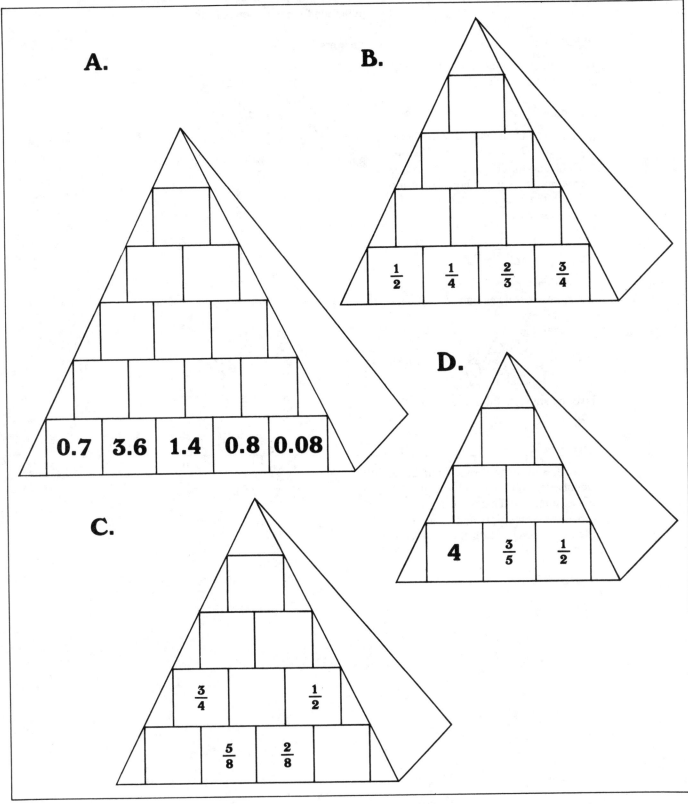

A.

0.7 | 3.6 | 1.4 | 0.8 | 0.08

B.

$\frac{1}{2}$ | $\frac{1}{4}$ | $\frac{2}{3}$ | $\frac{3}{4}$

C.

$\frac{3}{4}$ | $\frac{1}{2}$

$\frac{5}{8}$ | $\frac{2}{8}$

D.

4 | $\frac{3}{5}$ | $\frac{1}{2}$

For Teachers

MORE (PYRAMID) POWER TO YOU

Objective

To practice adding and subtracting decimals and common fractions

Directions

Explain to the students how the boxes in the pyramid faces are to be filled in. To find each number they must add the two numbers in the boxes right underneath the number.

For example:

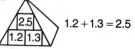

$1.2 + 1.3 = 2.5$

Ask students how they can find the missing number when one of the boxes underneath is empty.

For example:

$8 - 4.1 = 3.9$

Have the students fill in the rest of the numbers.

Extensions

1. Use the same worksheet, but have students multiply (or divide) to get the missing numbers. That is, each number is obtained by multiplying the numbers in the boxes underneath the number.

2. Have students make up their own pyramids for their friends to try.

Answers

A.
$$40.98$$
$$23.5 \qquad 17.48$$
$$16.3 \quad 7.2 \quad 10.28$$
$$11.3 \quad 5.0 \quad 2.2 \quad 8.08$$
$$0.7 \quad 3.6 \quad 1.4 \quad 0.8 \quad 0.08$$

B.
$$\frac{48}{12}$$
$$\frac{20}{12} \qquad \frac{28}{12}$$
$$\frac{3}{4} \qquad \frac{11}{12} \qquad \frac{17}{12}$$
$$\frac{1}{2} \qquad \frac{1}{4} \qquad \frac{2}{3} \qquad \frac{3}{4}$$

C.
$$\frac{24}{8}$$
$$\frac{13}{8} \qquad \frac{11}{8}$$
$$\frac{3}{4} \qquad \frac{7}{8} \qquad \frac{1}{2}$$
$$\frac{1}{8} \qquad \frac{5}{8} \qquad \frac{2}{8} \qquad \frac{2}{8}$$

D.
$$4\frac{17}{10}$$
$$4\frac{3}{5} \qquad \frac{11}{10}$$
$$4 \qquad \frac{3}{5} \qquad \frac{1}{2}$$

 Name_____

How many rectangles?

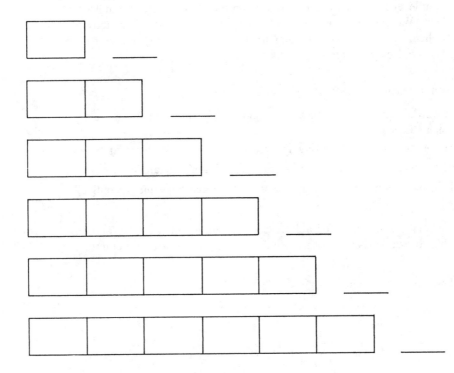

Complete the table.

Number of small rectangles	1	2	3	4	5	6	7	8	9	10
Total number of rectangles			6							

49

IDEAS

Objective: Experience with counting patterns

Comments: This set of experiences is nongraded. We have found that students from level 1 to level 8 enjoy working on the "How many rectangles?" activity sheet. We suggest that you start your students on the first activity sheet. Try them on each succeeding activity sheet until they experience frustration or show lack of interest.

Directions for teachers:

1. Remove the activity sheets that you decide to use and reproduce a copy for each student.

2. Start the students on counting the rectangles. Some students at every age level will have difficulty seeing the "composite" rectangles: and . Some will fail to count the "three-rectangle rectangle" .

3. Expect many students to be able to see the pattern in the table and to be able to extend their entries beyond those that were actually counted.

Answer keys and pattern clues:

Number of small (n)	1	2	3	4	5	6	7	8	9	10
Total number (t)	1	3	6	10	15	21	28	36	45	55

Pattern clues: The total number of rectangles (t) for any number of small rectangles (n) can be found by adding n to the total number for n − 1. (For 5 small rectangles, add 5 to the total of 4 small rectangles: 10 + 5 = 15.)

Rule: $t = \dfrac{n(n+1)}{2}$

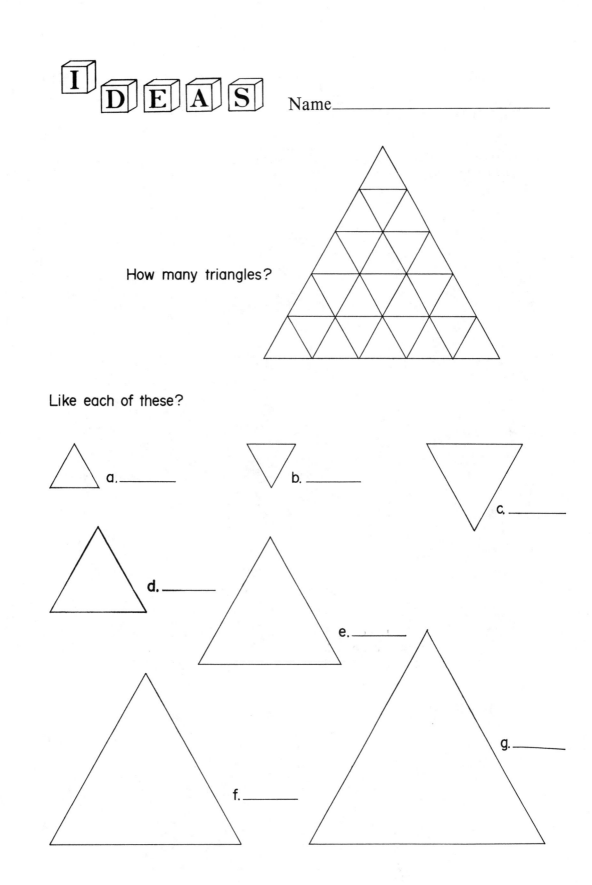

IDEAS

Name_____

How many triangles?

Like each of these?

a._____

b._____

c._____

d._____

e._____

f._____

g._____

IDEAS

a. $1 + 2 + 3 + 4 + 5 = 15$ b. $1 + 2 + 3 + 4 = 10$
c. $1 + 2 + 3 + 4 = 10$ d. $1 + 2 + 3 = 6$
e. $1 + 2 = 3$ f. $1 + 2 = 3$
g. 1

Suggestion: Ask your more pattern-conscious students to answer the same question for a large equilateral triangle with 6 $\triangle$'s in the bottom row.

How many squares?

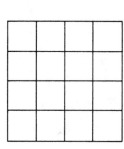

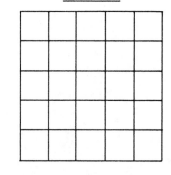

_____   _____   _____

_____   _____

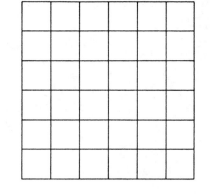

_____

Complete the table.

Number of rows	1	2	3	4	5	6	7	8
Number of small squares	1	4	9					
Total number of squares			14					

Rows (n)	1	2	3	4	5	6	7	8
Small	1	4	9	16	25	36	49	64
Total (t)	1	5	14	30	55	91	140	204

⬜ ⬜ ⬜ ⬜ ⬜ (IDEAS blocks)

Pattern clues: The total number of squares (t) for any number of rows of small squares (n) can be found by adding n^2 to the total for $(n - 1)$ rows. (For 6 rows, add 36 to the total for 5 rows: $36 + 55 = 91$.)

Rule: $t = n^2 + (n - 1)^2 + (n - 2)^2 + \cdots + (n - n)^2$

Name_____

What is the largest number of pieces of pie you can make with n cuts?

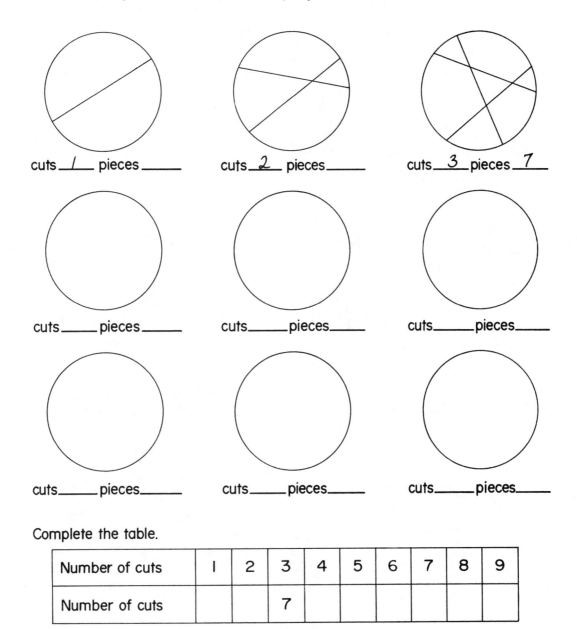

cuts _1_ pieces _____   cuts _2_ pieces _____   cuts _3_ pieces _7_

cuts _____ pieces _____   cuts _____ pieces _____   cuts _____ pieces _____

cuts _____ pieces _____   cuts _____ pieces _____   cuts _____ pieces _____

Complete the table.

Number of cuts	1	2	3	4	5	6	7	8	9
Number of cuts			7						

What is the largest number of pieces you can make with 20 cuts? _____

IDEAS

Cuts (n)	1	2	3	4	5	6	7	8	9
Pieces (p)	2	4	7	11	16	22	29	37	46

Pattern clues: The largest number of pieces for n cuts is n plus the number of pieces for $(n-1)$ cuts. (For 7 cuts you get $7 + 22$ pieces).

Rule: $p = \dfrac{n(n+1)}{2} + 1$

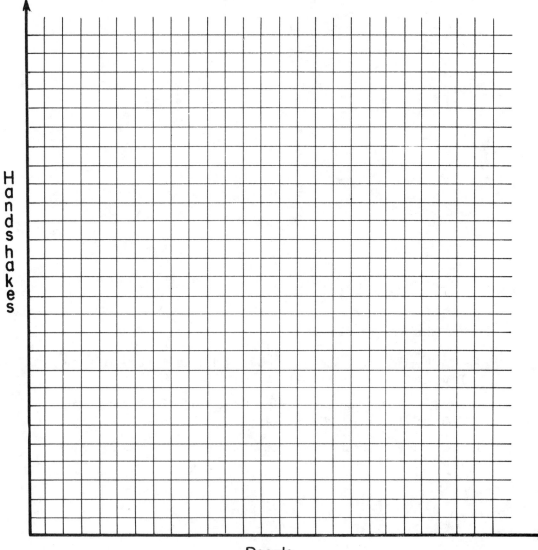

IDEAS

THE HANDSHAKE PATTERN

Suppose there were 10 people at a party and everyone shook hands with everyone else. How many hands handshakes would there be? A graph can help you see a pattern.

If there was 1 person, there would be 0 handshakes. With 2 people there would be 1 handshake. How many handshakes with 3 people? 4 people? 5 people? Fill in the chart and graph the number pairs.

How many handshakes would there be if everyone in your class shook hands with everyone else?

People	Shakes

Handshakes

People

Objectives: Experience with number pairs and graphs

Directions for teachers:

Duplicate a copy of the worksheet for each student. The problem on the worksheet is self-explanatory. The solution appears below.

People	Shakes
1	0
2	1
3	3
4	6
5	10
6	15
7	21
8	28
9	36
10	45

For other activities with graphs, see the following:

Bell, William R. "Cartesian Coordinates and Battleship." ARITHMETIC TEACHER 21 (May 1974): 421–22.

Good, Ronald G. "Two Mathematical Games with Dice." ARITHMETIC TEACHER 21 (January 1974): 45–47.

Liedtke, W.: "Geoboard Mathematics." ARITHMETIC TEACHER 21 (April 1974): 273–77

Take the number 7. If you had 7 squares of paper, there is only 1 way to make a rectangular shape

That's why 7 is colored on the chart

Try 12. There are several ways you can make a rectangle shape

Too many rectangles -- so 12 is not colored in

Investigate all the numbers on the chart and color those for which there is only 1 way to make a rectangle shape

1	2	3	4	5	6
7	8	9	10	11	12
13	14	15	16	17	18
19	20	21	22	23	24
25	26	27	28	29	30
31	32	33	34	35	36

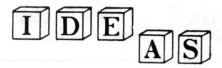

Objective: To investigate prime numbers

Directions for teachers:

1. Duplicate a worksheet for each student.
2. Make sure they understand the directions.

Going further:

1. Discuss prime numbers with your

For Teachers

class—all the prime numbers will be colored on the completed worksheets. A prime number has 2 distinct factors, itself and 1. Does the number 1 have two distinct factors? The number 1 is colored, but 1 is not a prime number.

2. Notice that all numbers colored below the first row appear in the 1 or 5 column. That's because the prime numbers, excepting 2 and 3, are 1 more or 1 less than a multiple of 6.

You are to put the numbers from 1 to 9 in the circles of each triangle

Put them here so that when you add up the numbers on each side, the three sums are all the same and the __smallest__ possible sum.

Put them here so that when you add up the numbers on each side, the three sums are all the same and the __largest__ possible sum.

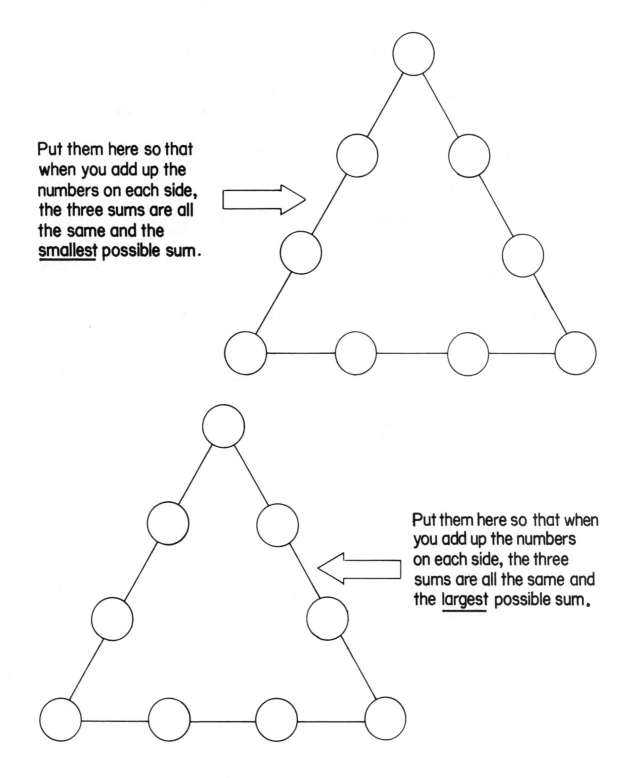

For Teachers

Objective: To provide drill in addition while solving a logical puzzle

Directions for teachers:

1. Duplicate a worksheet for each child.
2. Make sure they understand the directions.

Going further:

1. See if children can develop theories for how to solve the problem other than by trial and error.
2. Make up similar problems using other shapes and numbers of circles.

Answers:

Minimum sums

①
⑥ ⑨
⑧ ④
② ⑤ ⑦ ③

①
⑨ ⑦
⑤ ⑥
② ⑧ ④ ③

Maximum sums

⑨
⑤ ④
① ③
⑧ ② ⑥ ⑦

⑨
④ ⑥
② ①
⑧ ⑤ ③ ⑦

CONSECUTIVE NUMBER SUMS

Try to write all the numbers below as the sum of 2 or more consecutive numbers.

1 =

2 =

3 =

4 =

5 =

6 =

7 =

8 =

9 =

10 =

11 =

12 =

13 =

14 =

15 =

16 =

17 =

18 =

19 =

20 =

21 =

22 =

23 =

24 =

25 =

LOOK FOR PATTERNS!

Objective: To investigate number patterns

Directions for teachers:

1. Duplicate a worksheet for each child.
2. Make sure they understand the directions (especially the meaning of *consecutive*).

Going further:

1. You may extend the activity to 50. It's good addition reinforcement as well as giving the students a chance to use the patterns they've found. Sums for all the numbers except the powers of 2 (1, 2, 4, 8, 16, . . .) are possible.
2. How many different ways are there to write each number as the sum of consecutive numbers? For example:

$$7 + 8 = 15$$
$$4 + 5 + 6 = 15$$
$$1 + 2 + 3 + 4 + 5 = 15$$

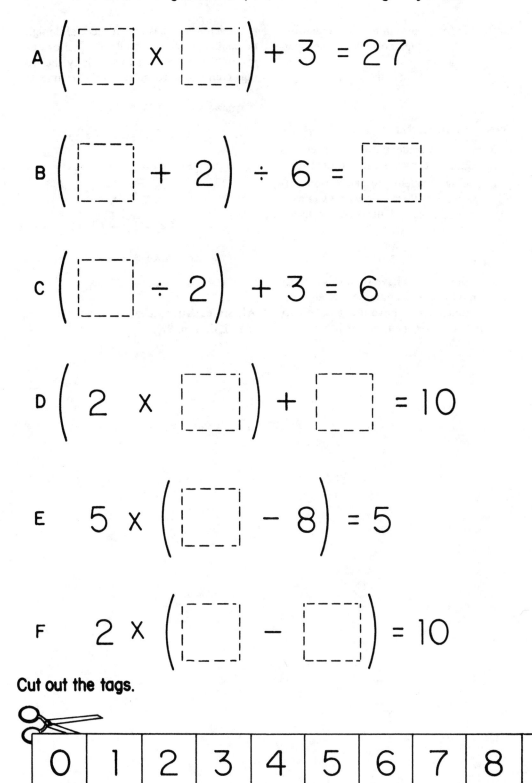

Match the number tags to the spaces. Use each tag only once.

A $\left(\boxed{} \times \boxed{} \right) + 3 = 27$

B $\left(\boxed{} + 2 \right) \div 6 = \boxed{}$

C $\left(\boxed{} \div 2 \right) + 3 = 6$

D $\left(2 \times \boxed{} \right) + \boxed{} = 10$

E $5 \times \left(\boxed{} - 8 \right) = 5$

F $2 \times \left(\boxed{} - \boxed{} \right) = 10$

Cut out the tags.

| 0 | 1 | 2 | 3 | 4 | 5 | 6 | 7 | 8 | 9 |

 For Teachers

Objective: Experience in building equations involving more than one operation

Directions for teachers:

1. Remove the student activity sheet and reproduce a copy for each student.
2. Encourage students to try various arrangements of their number tags so each tag is used once and all six equations are correct.

Comments:

After the students have tried this activity alone, modifications could be introduced:

The students who have not built all six equations could work together in pairs.

Students who have been successful might be challenged to build all six equations using only five tags. In this activity the five tags could be used more than one time.

Answers:

A (8×3) + 3 = 27

B (4 + 2) $\div$ 6 = 1

C ($6 \div 2$) + 3 = 6

D (2 $\times 5$) + 0 = 10

E 5 $\times$ (9 – 8) = 5

F 2 $\times$ (7 – 2) = 10

All six equations can be completed using tags 1, 2, 4, 6, 9.

Name _____

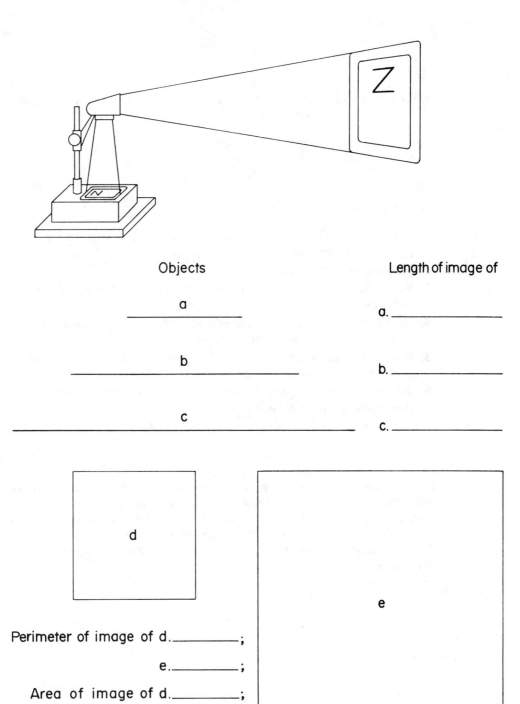

Objects

a _____

b _____

c _____

Length of image of

a. _____

b. _____

c. _____

Perimeter of image of d. _____;

e. _____;

Area of image of d. _____;

e. _____.

For Teachers

Objective: Experience in investigation of a physical geometry situation that involves constant ratio.

Directions for teachers:

1. Remove the activity sheet. Make a copy for each student and a transparency for your use.

2. Make sure that each student has a ruler.

3. Before class, set your projector so that the image of line segment a is 5 inches long.

4. Have each student measure segment a on his paper. Then have a volunteer measure its image on the screen (or chalkboard).

5. Have each student measure b on his paper. Then have each student guess how long the image of segment b is.

6. Repeat this process (step 5) with segment c and the perimeters and areas of the squares d and e.

Comments: The activity can be repeated with any desired setting of the projector. If the image of segment a is 10 times the length of a, then the image of segment b will be 10 times the length of b, and so on. The fact that segment b is twice the length of segment a, and that segment c is three times the length of segment a provides a second pattern for the student to investigate.

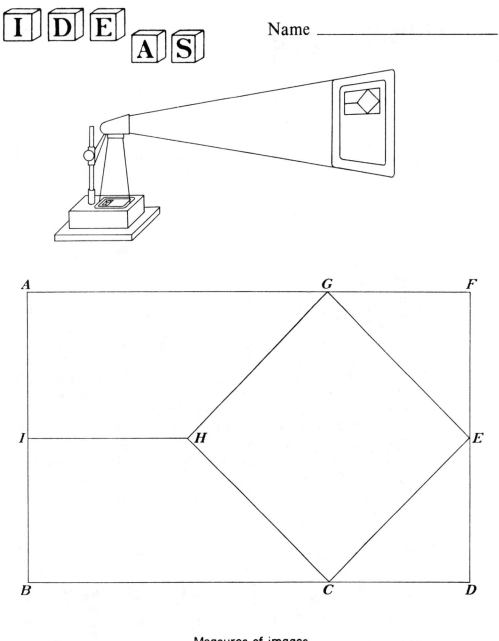

Name _____

Measures of images

Length	Angle measure	Perimeter	Area
$\overline{DF}$ _____	∠GFE _____	CEGH _____	ABDF _____
$\overline{FE}$ _____	∠FGE _____	ABDF _____	CEGH _____
$\overline{GE}$ _____	∠GHI _____	AGHI _____	
$\overline{FA}$ _____			
$\overline{AG}$ _____			

For Teachers

Objective: Experience in the investigation of a physical geometry situation that involves constant ratio and invariance of angle measure.

Directions for teachers:

1. Remove the activity sheet. Make a copy for each student and a transparency for your use.
2. Make sure that each student has a ruler and a protractor.
3. Before class, set your projector so that the image of segment $\overline{DF}$ on the screen (or chalkboard) is 14 inches long. (Avoid distortion of the figure by setting the projector on the same level as the screen.)
4. Have each student measure segment $\overline{DF}$ on his sheet. Then have a volunteer measure the image of $\overline{DF}$. Record the measure of the image.
5. Have each student complete the activity. Be sure that all students understand that only the measures of the image on the screen (or chalkboard) are recorded.
6. Discourage students from actually measuring the image lengths.

Note: You will need a chalkboard protractor.

Comments: The activity can be varied by changing the distance of the projector from the screen (or chalkboard). A discussion following the activity should bring out the patterns. The fact that the angle measure is constant will surprise many students.

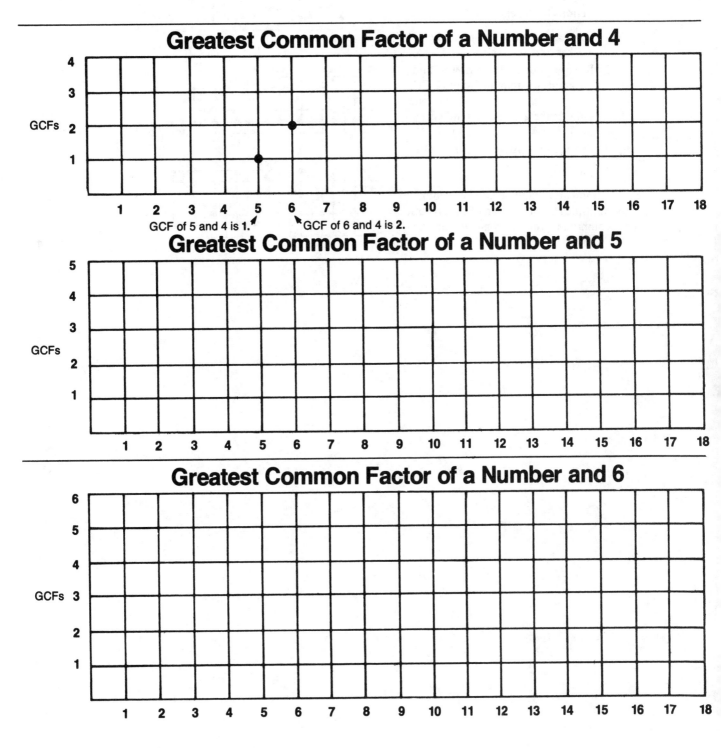

Name_____

For each graph, find the GCF of each of the numbers at the bottom of the graph with the number at the top of the graph. Graph each GCF. Two examples are done for you.
Do you see any patterns in your graph?

Greatest Common Factor of a Number and 4

GCFs

GCF of 5 and 4 is 1.   GCF of 6 and 4 is 2.

Greatest Common Factor of a Number and 5

GCFs

Greatest Common Factor of a Number and 6

GCFs

IDEAS For Teachers

Objective: To compute and graph the greatest common factor (GCF) of two numbers, and find patterns in the graphs.

Directions for teachers:

1. Give each student a copy of the worksheet.
2. Be sure students know how to find the greatest common factor (GCF). (The greatest common factor is the same as the greatest common divisor.)
3. Discuss the patterns in the graphs.

Going further:

Find and graph the least common multiple (LCM) instead of the greatest common factor. (Recognizing the patterns in the graphs is more difficult for LCM graphs than for GCF graphs.)

Answers:

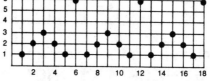

Computer Road Maps

Name _____

1. Follow the directions of the flowcharts below. What job did each have you do?

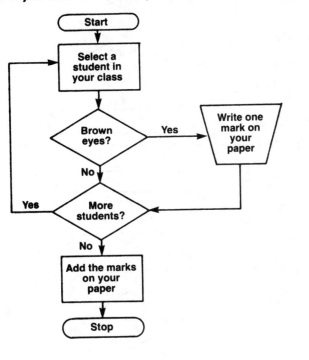

2. Fill in the flowchart below to give directions for writing the numbers from 1 to 10.

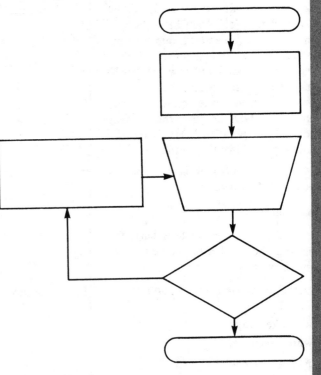

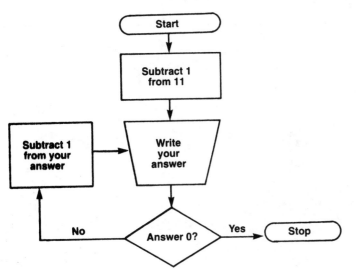

3. Match the flowchart symbols below with the kinds of messages they give.

Start, stop

Directions

Decision

Recording

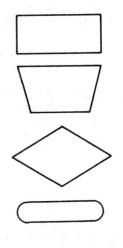

IDEAS for Using Flowcharts

COMPUTER ROAD MAPS

Objective

To introduce flowcharting

Materials

Worksheet and pencil

Directions

Discuss with the students the purpose of a flowchart and how a flowchart is analagous to a road map. Flowcharts show the computer the steps to follow to complete a job. Then have the students, working in small groups of four or five, follow the first flowchart. Discuss with the students how you could change the first decision box (Brown eyes?) to answer other questions—the number of boys or girls, the number older or younger than a certain age, the number who have pets, and so on.

Have the students complete the worksheets on their own.

Extensions

1. Have students make flowcharts for counting the number of people in their families with—

• birthdays in January, February, or March;

• who like sports;

• who drive cars;

• who are in school.

2. Have students suggest other characteristics that could be counted.

3. Have students make flowcharts that give directions for—

• writing the even numbers from 10 to 30;

• identifying the odd numbers between 45 and 57;

• finding the prime numbers up to 41;

• listing the things in the room that are shaped like a rectangle;

and so on.

Answers

(1) Write the numbers from 10 to 0, counting backwards.

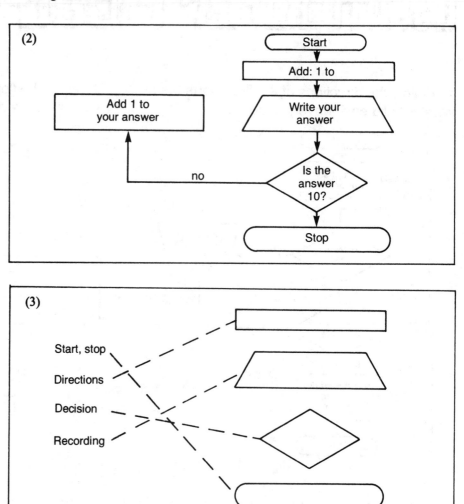

Program the Computer

Name _____

Sample: Forty-five students tried out for the team. Twenty-six were males. How many were females?

The program at the right tells the computer to subtract 26 from 45 to solve this problem.

Write computer programs for the following problems. The computer symbols for the operations are as follows: + (add), − (subtract), * (multiply), and / (divide).

10	**READ A, B**
20	**LET C = A − B**
30	**PRINT C**
40	**DATA 45, 26**
50	**END**

1. Five people each worked 23 hours on making the scenery for a play. How many hours did they work altogether?

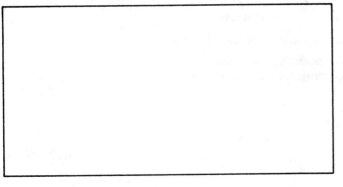

2. The school sold $354 worth of tickets at $3 each. How many tickets were sold?

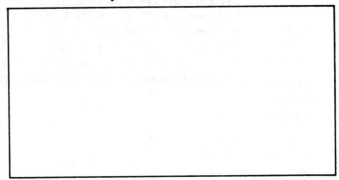

3. One hundred eight chairs were lined up in 4 rows. How many chairs were in each row?

4. Twenty-seven students are on the tennis team and 39 others are on the track team. How many students are on the track and tennis teams?

IDEAS

PROGRAM THE COMPUTER

Objective

An introduction to simple program writing to solve word problems.

Materials

Worksheet and pencil

Directions

Go over the sample problem and discuss the number sentence for solving it $(45 - 26 = \square)$. Read through the program that tells the computer how to solve the problem. Then have the students use that program for a model to tell the computer to subtract 12 from 25. Be certain that they note the changed order of the numbers (12, 25) in the program (DATA 25, 12). Review the computer symbols for the operations that are shown next. In particular, show how 24 divided by 3 (or 3 into 24) will be written 24/3. They can

proceed then to writing the programs for the rest of the problems.

Answers

All are the same as the sample except for the second and fourth lines:

1. 20 C = A * B
   40 5, 23

2. 20 C = A / B
   40 354, 3

3. 20 C = A / B
   40 108, 4

4. 20 C = A + B
   40 27, 39

Extensions

1. Introduce other symbols such as

   $\uparrow$, raise to a power

   ( ) , parentheses.

Make up more problems to solve.

2. If possible, have the students try their programs on a computer.

Fill in column *B* on the table by following the steps in the flowchart.

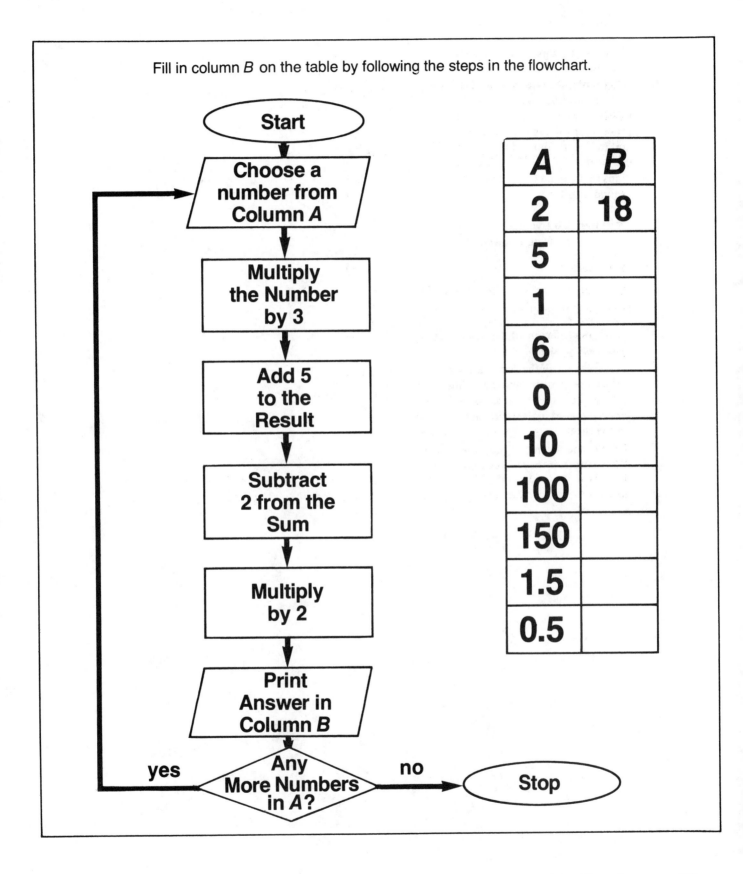

A	B
2	18
5	
1	
6	
0	
10	
100	
150	
1.5	
0.5	

IDEAS for this month consists of flowchart activities. A flowchart pictorially represents the steps necessary to perform specific tasks or to find solutions to problems. Each step in the process for solving a problem is listed and in a particular order. Flowcharts can be thought of as blueprints or maps that can be followed to reach a desired result.

Objective: To give students experience in using a flowchart.

Directions for teachers:

1. Provide a copy of the worksheet for each student.

2. Go through the flowchart with the class to insure understanding of the procedure. The first answer has been entered in the table on each worksheet.

3. For the seventh-eighth level, use calculators, if they are available.

Answers

18, 36, 12, 42, 6, 66, 606, 906, 15, 9

Name

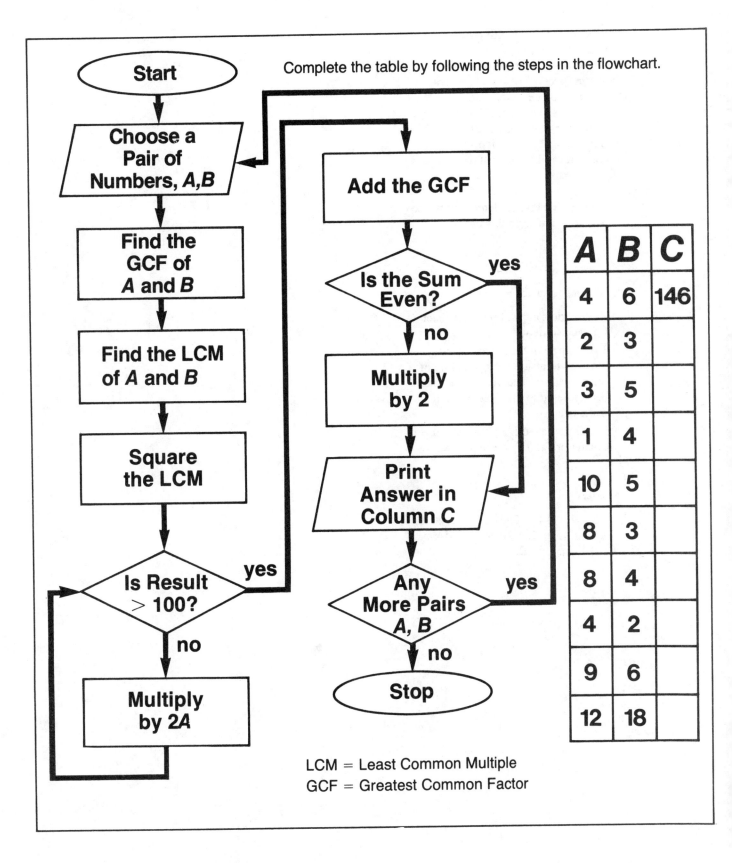

Complete the table by following the steps in the flowchart.

Start

Choose a Pair of Numbers, A,B

Find the GCF of A and B

Find the LCM of A and B

Square the LCM

Is Result > 100?

yes

no

Multiply by 2A

Add the GCF

Is the Sum Even?

yes

no

Multiply by 2

Print Answer in Column C

Any More Pairs A, B

yes

no

Stop

A	B	C
4	6	146
2	3	
3	5	
1	4	
10	5	
8	3	
8	4	
4	2	
9	6	
12	18	

LCM = Least Common Multiple
GCF = Greatest Common Factor

IDEAS for this month consists of flowchart activities. A flowchart pictorially represents the steps necessary to perform specific tasks or to find solutions to problems. Each step in the process for solving a problem is listed and in a particular order. Flowcharts can be thought of as blueprints or maps that can be followed to reach a desired result.

Objective: To give students experience in using a flowchart.

Directions for teachers:

1. Provide a copy of the worksheet for each student.

2. Go through the flowchart with the class to insure understanding of the procedure. The first answer has been entered in the table on each worksheet.

3. For the seventh-eighth level, use calculators, if they are available.

Answers

146, 290, 226, 258, 4010, 1154, 1028, 130, 654, 1302

Problem Solving Tic-Tac-Toe

Tic-Tac-Toe Board

Fill in the spaces on the Tic-Tac-Toe with these nine numbers.

2
3
4
6
38
60
77
81
108

Now choose any problem below. Solve it.
Put an *X* on the answer on the tic-tac-toe
board. You win when you get two tic-tac-toes.

Problems

I had 45 comic books. I gave my friend 24 of
them. My friend gave me 17 of her comic books.
How many comic books do I have now?

How many legs on 12 dogs and 15 cats?

How much money is 31 dimes and 18 nickels?

I bought 4 records at $4.25 each. I gave the
clerk $20. How much change did I receive?

How many hours in 3 days and 5 hours?

Roller coaster rides cost 25¢ each. Ferris

wheel rides cost 50¢ each. What's the cost for
four roller coaster rides and 2 ferris wheel
rides?

I had $20. I spent $2.50, $4.25, and $7.25. How
much is left?

How many legs on 9 cows and 12 chickens?

There are 4 teams of fifth graders and 5 teams
of sixth graders. Each team has 9 players. How
many players are there?

81

IDEAS

For Teachers

Objective: Experience in solving two-step addition, subtraction, and multiplication problems

Directions for teachers:

1. Remove the master and reproduce one copy for each student.

2. Students fill in their tic-tac-toe by randomly writing the numbers in the nine empty spaces.

3. Students choose any problem at the bottom of the page, solve it, and mark (X) the answer on their tac-tac-toe.

4. At the lower levels, students win with a simple tic-tac-toe (three Xs in a line vertically, horizontally, or diagonally). With older students, *two* tic-tac-toes (three Xs in a line twice) are needed to win.

Depending on your class, you may want to read the problems to your students. If the problems are read aloud, have the students select the order in which the problems are read.

The game may be played in partnerships. Players take turns selecting a problem, then mark their answer on the tic-tac-toe with either an X or O.

Problem Solving Tic-Tac-Toe

Fill in the spaces on the Tic-Tac-Toe with these nine numbers.

8
9
10
11
12
13
14
15
16

Tic-Tac-Toe Board

Now choose any problem below. Solve it. Put an *X* on the answer on the tic-tac-toe board. You win when you get two tic-tac-toes.

Problems

If you add 58 to my mystery number and then divide by 7, you get 10. What's my mystery number?

If you multiply my mystery number by 5 and then add 10, you get 75. What's my mystery number?

If you divide my mystery number by 7 and then add 18, you get 20. How old am I?

If you multiply my mystery number by 6 and then divide by 12, you get 4. What's my mystery number?

If you multiply my mystery number by 9 and then subtract 49, you get 50. What's my mystery number?

If you multiply my mystery number times itself and then add 19, you get 100. What's my mystery number?

Seven times my mystery number is 20 more than 5 times my mystery number. What's my mystery number?

My mystery number is between 10 and 20. If you divide it by 11, you get a remainder of 4. What's my mystery number?

If you divide my mystery number by 4 and then multiply by 10, you get 40. What's my mystery number?

Objective: Experience in solving two-
step addition, subtraction,
multiplication, and division
problems

Directions for teachers:

1. Remove the master and reproduce
   one copy for each student.
2. Students fill in their tic-tac-toe by
   randomly writing the numbers in
   the nine empty spaces.
3. Students choose any problem at the
   bottom of the page, solve it, and
   mark (X) the answer on their tac-
   tac-toe.
4. At the lower levels, students win
   with a simple tic-tac-toe (three Xs in
   a line vertically, horizontally, or diagonally). With older students, *two*
   tic-tac-toes (three Xs in a line twice)
   are needed to win.

   Depending on your class, you may
want to read the problems to your students. If the problems are read aloud,
have the students select the order in
which the problems are read.

   The game may be played in partnerships. Players take turns selecting a
problem, then mark their answer on
the tic-tac-toe with either an X or O.

Name _____

TREASURE JOURNEY

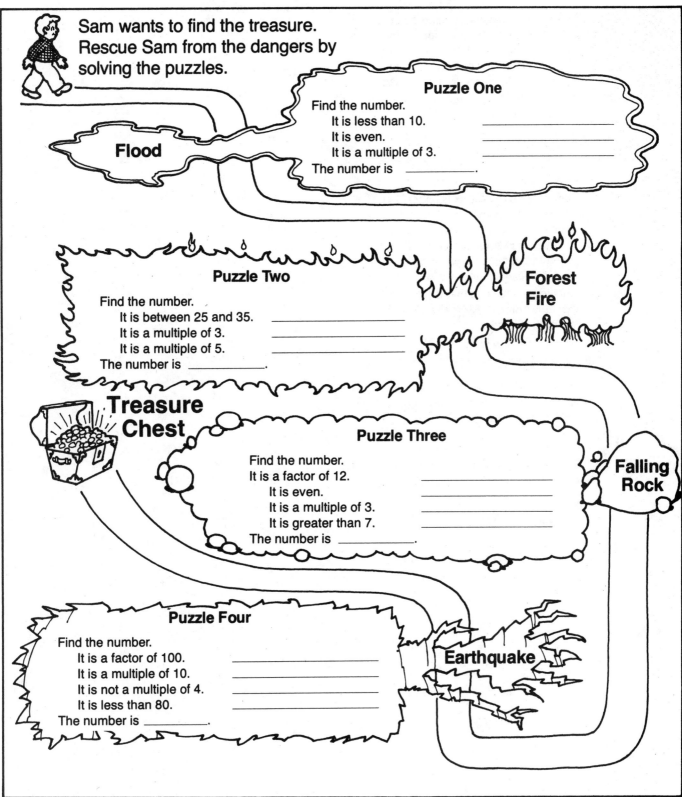

Sam wants to find the treasure.
Rescue Sam from the dangers by
solving the puzzles.

Flood

Puzzle One

Find the number.
   It is less than 10.   _____
   It is even.   _____
   It is a multiple of 3.   _____
The number is   _____.

**Forest
Fire**

Puzzle Two

Find the number.
   It is between 25 and 35. _____
   It is a multiple of 3. _____
   It is a multiple of 5. _____
The number is   _____.

**Treasure
Chest**

Puzzle Three

Find the number.
It is a factor of 12. _____
   It is even. _____
   It is a multiple of 3. _____
   It is greater than 7. _____
The number is   _____.

**Falling
Rock**

Puzzle Four

Find the number.
   It is a factor of 100. _____
   It is a multiple of 10. _____
   It is not a multiple of 4. _____
   It is less than 80. _____
The number is _____.

Earthquake

Treasure Journey

Objective: To provide students an opportunity to use logical reasoning with the concepts of
less than, greater than, multiple of, between, and factor
of.

Directions for teachers:

1. Give each student a copy of the
    worksheet.

2. Be sure that the students understand
    that for each puzzle, all the condi-
    tions must be satisfied simultane-
    ously. For example, in *Puzzle One*
    the number must be less than ten
    and even *and* a multiple of 3.

3. Suggest to students that they list the
    possible numbers for each clue. For
    example, for *Puzzle One* the stu-
    dent's work might look like this:

It is less than 10.

<u>1, 2, 3, 4, 5, 6, 7, 8, 9</u> (Only positive

It is even.   whole numbers

<u> 2,   4,   6,   8 </u> are used.)

It is a multiple of 3.

<u>   6   </u>

The number is <u>6</u>.

Answers:
One, 6; Two, 30; Three, 12; Four, 10

Going further:
Have students make puzzles like these.

Name _____

SERIOUS MYSTERIOUS CLUES

B. It is a multiple of 3.
C. It is a multiple of 4.
D. It is a multiple of 5.
E. It is less than 20.
H. It is a factor of 64.
J. It is not even.

N. It is even.
O. It is greater than 20.
P. It is not a multiple of 10.
R. It is not a multiple of 4.
T. It is a factor of 100.
U. It is less than 10.

Use the clues under the magnifying glass to identify each mystery number.
Use as few clues as possible.
The letters associated with the clues form a word.

1. The number is 15.
    Clues: _____
    _____
    _____

2. The number is 4.
    Clues: _____
    _____
    _____

3. The number is 25.
    Clues: _____
    _____
    _____
    _____

4. The number is 50.
    Clues: _____
    _____
    _____
    _____
    _____

5. The number is 8.
    Clues: _____
    _____
    _____
    _____

Serious Mysterious Clues

Objectives: To provide students an opportunity to use logical reasoning with the concepts of multiple of, less than, greater than, and factor of.

Directions for teachers:

1. Give each student a copy of the worksheet.
2. Emphasize that the puzzle should use as few clues as possible and that the clues apply only to positive whole numbers.
3. Let the students work the puzzles they have made.

Answers:
1. B, D, E   (BED)
2. C, T, U   (CUT)
3. T, O, P   (TOP) The order of the clues is important.
4. N, O, R, T (TORN)
5. There is no answer. The closest one can get is C, U which leaves 4 and 8 as possible answers. The clues that are given do not provide enough conditions to eliminate the number 4. When students tell you they can't make a puzzle, suggest that they make up another clue to use; for example, it is not a factor of 100.

Team _____

_____

_____

_____

Solve these problems:

1. One time John paid $.35 a gallon for gas. His tank holds 20 gallons of gas. John now pays $.45 a gallon. How much more does he pay for a tank of gas?— *Valerie Schiefer, grade 5, E. W. Chittum Elementary School, Chesapeake, Virginia.*

2. What is the surface area of a box that fits tightly around a plate with a radius of 6″ and a 3″ thickness?—*Jeff Ullman, grade 6, Harmar School, Marietta, Ohio.*

3. My mother baked Toll House cookies last night. She had 50 rows of cookies with 15 cookies in each row. How many cookies did she have in all?—*Freida Kavouras, grade 5, Adams School, Vandergrift, Pennsylvania.*

4. If Frank bought 92 acres of land at 534 dollars an acre and after 20 years he sold half of his 92 acres of land at 2,174 dollars an acre, how much profit did Frank make?—*Patty Seward, grade 6, Orchard Road School, Skillman, New Jersey.*

5. Joe collected _____ bottles. At 7¢ for every 3 bottles, he earned $9.24. How many bottles did he collect?—*Chris Leidig, grade 6, Southeastern Elementary School, Chesapeake, Virginia.*

6. Jim had 23,000 baseball cards. Joe had 2,100 baseball cards. How many cards did Jim have more than Joe?—*Jimmy Grisafe, grade 4, Pershing School, Berwyn, Illinois.*

7. One day Bazil ran 2,880 feet. If Bazil ran a yard more everyday in a week, how many feet will he have run?—*Julia Powell, grade 5, Barrington, Illinois.*

8. From Monday through Friday, each day the people were admitted into the Memorial Hospital: Monday, 50; Tuesday, 51; Wednesday, 49; Thursday, 48; Friday, 55; Saturday, 52; Sunday, 47. (a) What is the median? (b) What is the range? (c) What is the average?—*Dianna Biehl, grade 6, Harmar School, Marietta, Ohio.*

9. Joe drove from Norfolk to Los Angeles, which is 3400 miles. Joe purchased 200 gallons of gas during the trip. Joe made ten stops, and bought an equal amount of gas at each stop. How much gas was bought at each stop? What was Joe's mileage per gallon of gas?—*Jimmy Daffron, grade 6, Southeastern Elementary School, Chesapeake, Virginia.*

10. A Cadillac gets 9 miles to the gallon. A Volkswagen gets 32 miles to the gallon. A motorcycle gets 75 miles to the gallon. Gas costs 50 cents a gallon. If you went 726 miles, how much would you save by driving a motorcycle?— *Brian Cummins, grade 5, Orchard Road School, Skillman, New Jersey.*

11. Joe had 12 apples left over. He gave 4 to Mary and 3 to Ricky; then Ricky gave 2 away. Then Joe got 1053 more apples and he's selling them at 5¢ apiece. 267 were rotten. How much money did he lose and how many apples does he have left over, including those from the start?—*Charles Tripp, ungraded, Chesapeake Demonstration School, Chesapeake, Virginia.*

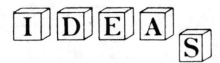 For Teachers

Objective: Experience in solving problems that were authored by other students.

Directions:

1. Remove the activity sheets and reproduce a copy for each student.
2. Have your students work independently for half of the period.
3. Have your students work in teams of four students each for the remainder of the period.
4. Collect one set of solutions from each team.
5. You may wish to post the results on the three "top" teams.

Comments: Your students may be critical of the wording of problems. Encourage them to improve on these problems and to write problems of their own. A "Problem of the Week" posted weekly on the bulletin board is a popular and self-motivation project.

Team _____

_____

_____

_____

Solve these problems:

1. Jim bought 3 notebooks, which cost $.59 each; 5 pencils, which were $.10 each; and 1 package of notebook paper for $3.96. He handed the clerk 7 pieces of money equalling the exact change. What were they?—*Steven Wingfield, grade 7, Hazelwood Junior High, Florissant, Missouri.*

2. The following is a portion of a report submitted by an investigator for a well-known market analysis agency with standards of accuracy so high that it boasts that an employee's first mistake is his last one.

Number of consumers interviewed	100
Number who drink coffee	78
Number who drink tea	71
Number who drink coffee and tea	48

   Why was the interviewer discharged?—*Susan Gardner, North Washington School, Apollo, Pennsylvania.*

3. Jim was an antique collector. He went to a sale in March 1972. At this sale he bought 75 salts. He paid 17 cents apiece for them. These salts were approximately 75 years old. Objects like this increase (on the average) 2.5 cents every 3 years. If Jim is now 13 years old and he keeps the salts until he is 75, how much will they be worth?—*Kevin Dean, grade 9, Bridge Street School, Wheeling, West Virginia.*

4. One foot of rail of a railroad track weighs 25 lbs. A length of rail is 30 feet long. Naturally a train needs two rails to run on. How much does a set of lengths weigh? The distance from Morris Plains to Hoboken is 37.5 miles as the train rolls. How many tons does the track weigh between the two stations?—*Cynde Catizone, grade 7, Morris Plains School, Morris Plains, New Jersey.*

5. If the Johns family lived 97 miles away from town and had a 20-gallon tank on their car and got 4 miles per gallon, how many times could they make it to town and back on 4½ tanks?—*Mark Brown, grade 8, Jefferson Junior High, Mattoon, Illinois.*

6. You are building a house. You need 9 yards of cement (1 yard costs $6.75), 3 doors (1 door costs $11.07), 11 windows (2 for $25.00), and 100 bricks ($.75 each). How much will all this cost, with $.03 tax on every dollar?—*Patty Caldwell, grade 7, Bridge Street School, Wheeling, West Virginia.*

7. If one man can do 301 push-ups in a week, and another 225, what would be the total of both in a month?—*George Thompson, grade 7, Van Sickle Junior High, Springfield, Massachusetts.*

8. A machine produces 160 jars per minute, 100 short jars and 60 tall jars. The tall jars are 6″ tall and the short jars are 3″ tall. The machine breaks 4 short jars and 1 tall jar every minute and it takes 20 seconds to clean up the glass. Suppose the machine produced at a normal rate of 7 days a week, breaking the usual number of jars: (a) If, after 3 weeks, all the jars were laid end to end, how long would the line of jars be? in inches? in feet? in yards? (b) How much time would be needed to make 1,007,735 long and short jars?—*Rowland Staton, grade 6, E. W. Chittum Elementary, Chesapeake, Virginia.*

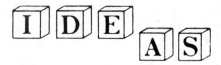

For Teachers

Objective: Experience in solving problems that were authored by other students.

Directions:

1. Remove the activity sheets and reproduce a copy for each student.
2. Have your students work independently for half of the period.
3. Have your students work in teams of four students each for the remainder of the period.
4. Collect one set of solutions from each team.
5. You may wish to post the results on the three "top" teams.

Comments: Your students may be critical of the wording of problems. Encourage them to improve on these problems and to write problems of their own. A "Problem of the Week" posted weekly on the bulletin board is a popular and self-motivation project.

Name_____

Solve the following problems if enough information is given. If not enough information is given, state what is needed.

1. Bill bought 3 model airplanes at $1.79 each and 2 model cars at $1.49 each. What was the total cost excluding tax?

2. Elaine bought 6 cans of cat food at $.35 each. How much change did she receive from the clerk?

3. The temperature at noon was below freezing. In 2 hours, it dropped another 4°. What was the temperature at 2 p.m.?

4. What is the area of this rectangular region?

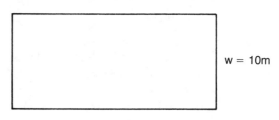

w = 10m

l = 24m

5. A triangle has an area of 140 square centimeters. What is the length of its base?

6. Maria works at a grocery store after school and earns $2.50 per hour. What does she earn per week?

7. Forty five percent of the graduating class at King Elementary were girls. If there were 80 graduates, how many boys were there?

8. Ben bought a record for $7.95 and a tape for $5.95. Sales tax was 5%. What was the total bill?

9. A company manufacturers metal rods that are 1.5 meters long and weigh 2.5 kg. What is the total weight of a box of these metal rods?

10. Alice shares a paper route with her brother by delivering on alternate days. They deliver the same number of papers daily and their weekly total is 350. How many does Alice deliver each week?

IDEAS For Teachers

Objective: Experience in identifying problems with insufficient data and in providing appropriate needed data.

Directions for teachers:

1. Reproduce one worksheet for each student.

2. Explain to students that in some problems more information than is given is necessary to solve the problems. If sufficient information is given in the problem, then they are to solve the problem. If the given information is not enough, they are to state what is needed.

3. Go over the results with the class.

Going further:

1. Elicit from the class sets of problems in which some of the problems cannot be solved without additional information.

2. In real life it is also common to encounter problem situations where there is an abundance of information. Students need to develop skill in choosing those facts that are needed to solve a problem in which there is extra information. Provide practice in working with problems with abundant information.

Answers

1. $8.35

2. More information needed. How much money to the clerk?

3. More information needed. What was temperature at noon?

4. 240 square meters

5. Need to know length of altitude of triangle.

6. Need to know total hours worked per week.

7. 44 boys

8. $14.60

9. Need to know number of rods in a box

10. Need to know number of days worked by Alice; 4 days or 3 days

Name _____

Find a way to determine the sum of the first **n** odd numbers. Do these to get you started:

$1 + 3 = ?$

$1 + 3 + 5 = ?$

$1 + 3 + 5 + 7 + 9 + 11 + 13 + 15 + 17 + 19 + 21 = ?$

$5!$

If 5! means $5 \times 4 \times 3 \times 2 \times 1$, how many terminal zeros will you have if you compute 10!? 100!?

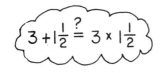

Can you find numbers **x** and **y** such that $x + y = x \cdot y$? How many pairs are counting numbers? How many are fractions? Try $x + y + z = x \cdot y \cdot z$.

Put 9 pigs in 4 pens so there are an odd number of pigs in each pen.

If one side of a triangle measures 4 cm, and if **x** and **y** are the measures of the other two sides, can **x** and **y** be any numbers? For example, if $x = 4$, could $y = 1$? $y = 2$? $y = 3$? $y = 4$? $y = 5$? $y = 6$? $y = 7$? $y = 8$? $y = 9$? If $x = 3$, could $y = 1$? $y = 2$? $y = 3$? $y = 4$? $y = 5$? $y = 6$? $y = 7$? $y = 8$? Try other values of **x** and **y**. Put in a table all of the pairs of **x** and **y** that make a triangle with the third side equal to 4. Do you see any patterns in the table? If you use the values of **x** and **y** in your table as coordinates of points, and if you graph the points, can you see any patterns in your graph?

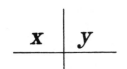

x	y

Objective: Experiences in problem solving

Directions for teachers: (all levels)

1. Remove the activity sheet and make a copy of it.
2. Cut the problems apart and paste each one on a 5-by-7 card.
3. Suggestions for use:

    a. Post one as the "Problem of the Week." Post student solutions with next week's problem.

    b. Give one to each team of students. Have teams report their progress or solution.

    c. Give one to an individual as a special challenge or a special project.

Comments: Be receptive to partial solutions and incomplete reasoning patterns. Encourage students to test their ideas. Open-ended problems such as these often suggest other problems to the perceptive student. Encourage your students to create problems for your file.

Answer Key

—$1 + 3 = 4 = 2^2$, 2 odd numbers; $1 + 3 + 5 = 9 = 3^2$, 3 odd numbers; $1 + 3 + 5 + 7 = 16 = 4^2$, 4 odd numbers; $1 + 3 + 5 + 7 \ldots = n^2$, n odd numbers.

—10!, 2 zeros; 100!, 21 zeros.

—Two pairs of counting numbers, (0, 0) and (2, 2); an endless set of fractions (4, 4/3), (5, 5/4), (6, 6/5), . . .

—Three pens each have 3 pigs. The large pen has 9 pigs.

—In the table, $x + y > 4$, or $x - y < 4$.

On the graph, the points determined by the pairs (x, y) fall in the shaded region. The points on the dotted line are pairs (x, y) for isosceles triangles. The point marked by $\times$, (4, 4), is the pair for an equilateral triangle.

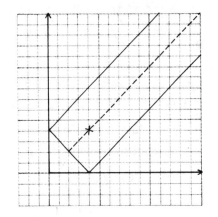

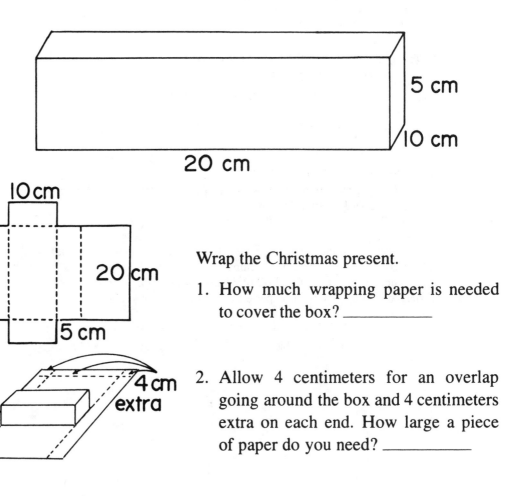

IDEAS

Partners _____

_____

Wrap the Christmas present.

1. How much wrapping paper is needed to cover the box? _____

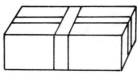

2. Allow 4 centimeters for an overlap going around the box and 4 centimeters extra on each end. How large a piece of paper do you need? _____

3. Tie it with a ribbon. How long a ribbon do you need to go around both ways?

   _____

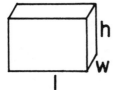

4. Allow 50 centimeters for a bow. How much ribbon do you need? _____

Research Problem: Work out a rule for the amount of paper needed to wrap any box (allow a 4 cm. overlap and ³/₄h. on each side to cover the ends).

 For Teachers

Objective: Experience with problem solving involving area and distance around an object.

Directions for teachers:

1. Remove the activity sheet and reproduce a copy for each student.
2. Have the students work in pairs.
3. Provide ¼-inch or ½-inch graph paper for those that need to make a model or do a layout of the model.
4. Post solutions to the "Research Problem."

Comments: Problem solving is the primary purpose of mathematics. As our curricula move toward an empahsis on applied mathematics, we will experience an increased focus on problem-solving skills. Children need a wide variety of problem-solving experiences to build their skills.

Key: 1. 700 sq. cm. 2. 28 cm. by 34 cm. or 952 sq. cm. 3. 80 cm. 4. 130 cm. Research Problem: $(2w + 2h + 4)$ by $(l + 3/2h)$

Name _____

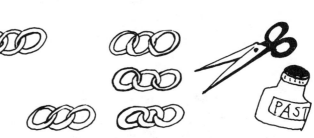

1. How many links do you need to cut and paste together to make one 15 link "chain" out of these 5 pieces? _____

2. How can you give one of these four presents to each of 4 girls so that one present is left in the box? _____

3. A boy bought one present for each of his sisters. He also bought one present for each of his brothers. He bought as many presents for brothers as he did for sisters. His sister also bought one present for each. She bought only half as many presents for sisters as she did for brothers. How many brothers does he have?

_____

4. The present belongs to Bill, Ed, or Jon. Whose present is it? _____

   These statements are true:
   1. The present belongs to Bill or Ed.
   2. The present belongs to Ed or Jon.
   3. The present does not belong to Jon.

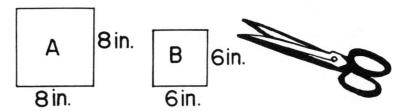

Cut squares A and B each into 2 pieces. Fit the 4 pieces together to form one 10 inch by 10 inch square.

 For Teachers

Objective: Problem-solving experiences that encourage the students to employ a variety of methods of solution.

Directions for teachers:

1. Remove the activity sheet and reproduce a copy for each student.
2. Present these problems as a challenge. Seek a variety of solutions rather than "the" answers.
3. Be as receptive to good thinking and innovative approaches as correct solutions.
4. Post detailed written solutions or have successful students explain their solutions to others.

Comments: Neither encourage nor discourage students working collectively on these problems. They present a level of challenge that is best approached through the student's chosen learning style.

Key:

1. Three links need to be cut.

2. Give a present to each of 3 girls, then give the box with the remaining present to the fourth girl.
3. 3 brothers (also 3 sisters)
4. Ed. (Several reasoning patterns are possible.)

5. (Other solutions are possible.)

IDEAS

How Long Would It Take You to Tear a Piece of Paper For Everyone in The United States?

Conduct an experiment.

Time yourself for one minute. How many pieces of paper can you tear in one minute?

_____

At this rate, how many pieces could you tear in one hour? _____

How long would it take you to tear a piece of paper for everyone in the United States (220,000,000 people)? _____

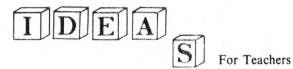 For Teachers

Objective: Experience in problem solving using large numbers

Directions for teachers:

1. Remove the activity sheet and reproduce a copy for each student.
2. To solve the problem, have students conduct an experiment by following the directions.

Comments:

If calculators are available, students should be encouraged to use them. The main focus of this activity is on problem solving rather than computation.

Name _____

Name _____

1. Choose a page from the phone book.

2. Write down the sum of the last two digits of 50 telephone numbers. 266-72⑰ → 8

Trials

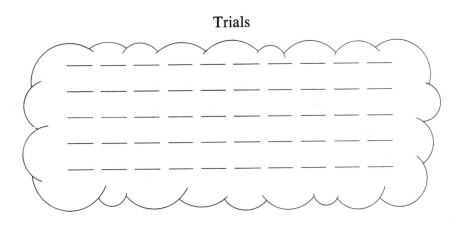

Sum	Tally	Total
0		
1		
2		
3		
4		
5		
6		
7		
8		
9		

Sum	Tally	Total
10		
11		
12		
13		
14		
15		
16		
17		
18		
19		

For Teachers

Objective: Experience in reading data.

Directions for teachers:

1. Remove the student worksheet and reproduce one copy for each pair of students.
2. Cut out a page of an outdated telephone book for each pair of students.
3. Have students read phone numbers and identify last two digits, and put the sums on the blackboard.

Directions for students:

1. You are to work in pairs.
2. Each pair should mark 50 numbers in a row on your page of the phone book.
3. List the sum of the last two digits on the blanks on your worksheet.
4. Make a tally for each sum in the table and find the totals.

Comments: Many students may need some instruction when it comes to tallying their data. You may want to stop the activity when the students reach this point and explain this technique. Depending upon the level of your class, you may want to discuss the most likely sum, the average, the median, or the mode of the resulting frequency. You may also want to compile a class frequency from the individual data. Most students will be anxious to explain why no tally marks appear after "19."

HOW OFTEN ARE LETTERS USED?

The letter of the alphabet used most often in English is the letter E. Then came T, A, O, and N. Those used least are Q, Z, K, X, J.

Test this theory. Find any three sentences in a book and tally each letter below. Compare your results with your classmates.

a   n

b   o

c   p

d   q

e   r

f   s

g   t

h   u

i   v

j   w

k   x

l   y

m   z

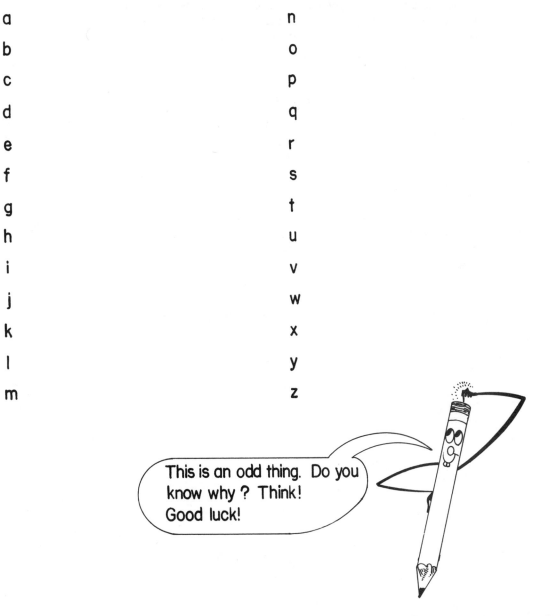

This is an odd thing. Do you know why? Think! Good luck!

 **IDEAS**

"Mathematizing the Alphabet" is the theme for this month's IDEAS section. The activities are presented in a sequence starting with the simpler investigations. Levels are indicated for your general use, but choose the worksheets that best suit your own students.

Duplicate the worksheets you choose for your students. Perhaps you can use the ideas to set up a learning center on "Mathematizing the Alphabet." Assign one or two worksheets for the students and let them choose one or two others to try. Incorporate other disciplines by having children investigate alphabets of other cultures, compare decorative alphabets used in various books and advertisements, create alphabets of their own.

The activities are self-explanatory. Make sure the students understand the directions before they start.

Answers:

^{I}DEAS   There is no "E" in the balloon.

Circle your answer to each of the following questions:

1. Is it likely or unlikely that two people in your class have a birthday during the same month?   Likely   Unlikely

2. Is it likely or unlikely that two people in your class have a birthday during the same week?   Likely   Unlikely

3. Is it likely or unlikely that two people in your class have the same birthday?   Likely   Unlikely

Be able to defend your decision in each case.

Record the birthdays of the members of your class on a 12-month calendar.

Answer the following questions:

1. Did two people have a birthday in the same month?   Yes   No

2. Did two people have a birthday during the same week?   Yes   No

3. Did two people have the same birthday?   Yes   No

4. If you did this same thing for another class, how would you answer the three questions for that group? Would your answers be the same?

5. If you did the same thing for the whole school, would your answers still be the same? Explain why your answers would or would not be the same.

6. Do you think there would be any chance that as many as five people might have the same birthday in your class? In the school? How did you decide?

COMMON BIRTHDAYS

Objective

To predict the occurrence of events on the basis of whether they are likely or unlikely and then test the predictions.

Directions

1. Distribute a worksheet to each student.

2. Have students answer the questions in the first part of the worksheet.

3. On a 1981 calendar, circle the dates of the birthdays of the members of the class.

4. Discuss the answers to the questions in the second part of the worksheet.

5. Have students answer the questions in the third part of the worksheet.

6. Discuss with the students their answers to the questions in the third part.

Extensions

Repeat the activity with other groups and with groups of other sizes. For example, try the experiment in other classes, for all the students in one grade level, or for all the students in the school.

Name _____

Use only the points below as corners:

Draw a square whose area is 16 square centimeters.

Draw a rectangle whose area is 33 square centimeters.

Draw the largest square you can. What is it's area ?_____

Use the points below to draw 3 squares.

Name them . _____ , _____ , _____ .

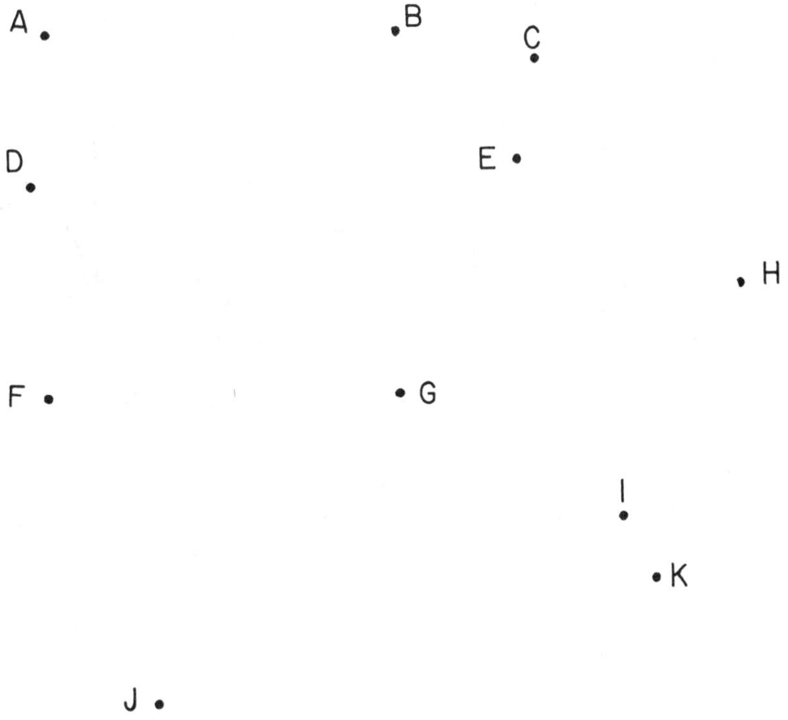

A .

.B

C .

D .

E .

. H

F .

. G

I .

. K

J .

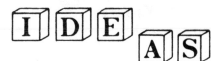

For Teachers

Objective: Experience in visualizing specific geometric objects

Directions for teachers:

1. Remove the activity sheet and reproduce a copy for each student.
2. Be sure each student has a centimeter rule.
3. As you observe students working, be sure they understand that only the given points can be used as "corners" and that not all points need to be used.

Comments: Since it is *not* the purpose of this activity to teach the concepts, care should be taken that this sheet is used only after the student has studied the area of squares and rectangles using metric measures.

Key:

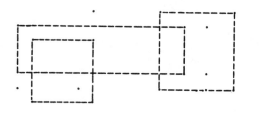

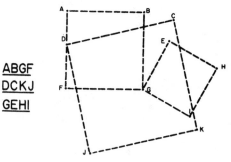

ABGF
DCKJ
GEHI

Name _____

Use the points below as corners

    Draw two congruent rectangles.

    Draw two congruent <u>obtuse</u> triangles.

Use the points below as corners

    Draw two rectangles with equal areas.

    Draw two congruent <u>acute</u> triangles.

Objective: Experience in visualizing geometric objects with specific characteristics

Directions for teachers:

1. Remove the activity sheet and reproduce a copy for each student.
2. Be sure that each student has a straightedge but do not require that he use it.
3. Have students work independently.

Comments: The activities can be made considerably more challenging by having your students try to find the congruent triangles *before* they draw the rectangles or by adding one or two extraneous points. The latter must be done very carefully so that other pairs of solutions are not introduced.

Key:

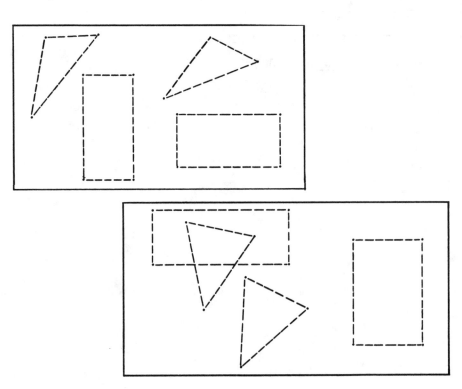

Cut out these pieces and make two squares.

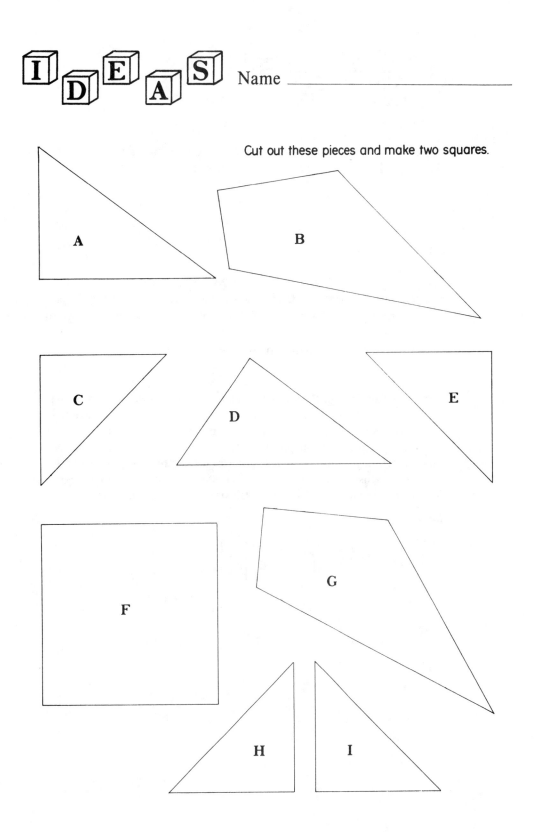

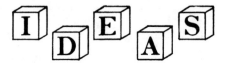 For Teachers

Objective: Experience in constructing a square from a variety of polygons, each containing at least one right angle

Directions for teachers:

1. Remove the activity sheet and reproduce a copy for each student.
2. Be sure students understand that they are to use all nine pieces in forming the two squares. (Polygon *F* is not one of the two squares they are to form!)
3. Encourage the students to work independently.

Comments: Though this activity could easily be viewed simply as a puzzle, it is far more than that. The student who struggles with this activity has personal experience with the basic concepts of congruence and tessellations. The fact that the solution produces two squares that are the same size has important though subtle implications for the sophisticated concept of area. A skillful discussion leader may be successful in drawing out many generalizations from the students if he doesn't insist on precise language.

Solution

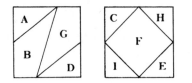

IDEAS

BOXING SQUARES

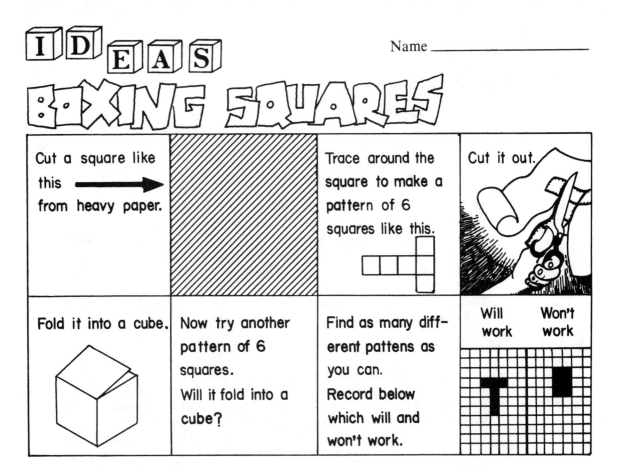

Cut a square like this ➡️ from heavy paper.

Trace around the square to make a pattern of 6 squares like this.

Cut it out.

Fold it into a cube.

Now try another pattern of 6 squares.
Will it fold into a cube?

Find as many different pattens as you can.
Record below which will and won't work.

Will work   Won't work

Will work.							

Won't work.						

IDEAS

For Teachers

Boxing Squares

See:

Maletsky, Evan M. "Activities: Patterns and Positions." MATHEMATICS TEACHER 66 (December 1973): 723–26.

Walter, Marion I. "A Second Example of Informal Geometry: Milk Cartons." In *Readings in Geometry from the ARITHMETIC TEACHER,* edited by Marguerite Brydegaard and James E. Inskeep, Jr., pp. 48–50. Washington, D.C.: National Council of Teachers of Mathematics, 1970.

Walter, Marion I. *Boxes, Squares and Other Things.* Washington, D.C.: The National Council of Teachers of Mathematics, 1971.

Going further:

To extend this month's theme, have your students use their investigations as the contents for individual project books on squares. Each project book will need a cover of construction paper (square in shape, of course). The activity sheets can be the basic content, along with whatever else you and your students find appropriate. Include a creative writing assignment, "If I Were a Square" or "A World without Squares." Look in the school library for books about squares. Have students compile lists of square shapes that they see in their homes, or on the way to school—What foods do we eat that are square in shape?

Investigating the elegance of the square is a worthwhile mathematical endeavor in itself, but its richness can be expanded to relate to the real world so children can see mathematics as other than an isolated subject that they study in school.

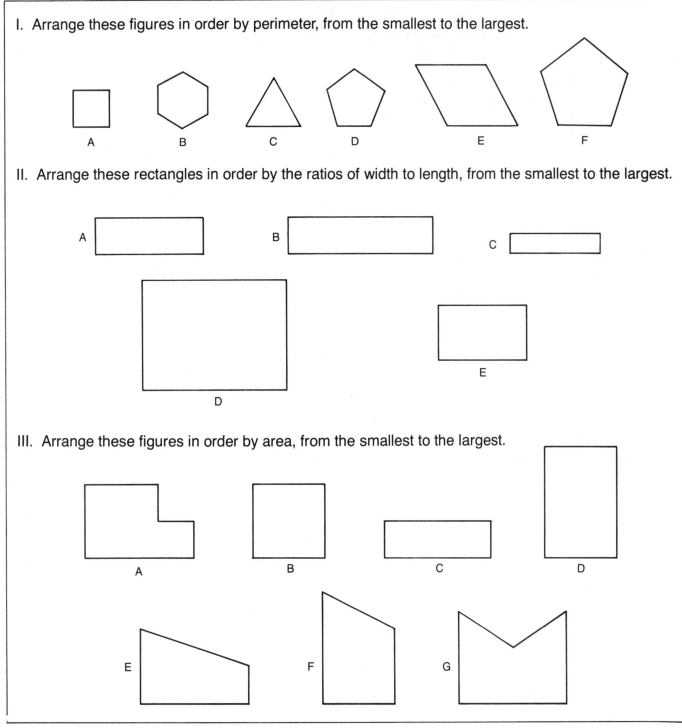

Onward and Upward

I. Arrange these figures in order by perimeter, from the smallest to the largest.

A   B   C   D   E   F

II. Arrange these rectangles in order by the ratios of width to length, from the smallest to the largest.

A   B   C

D   E

III. Arrange these figures in order by area, from the smallest to the largest.

A   B   C   D

E   F   G

IDEAS For Teachers

Objectives: Experiences in measuring with metric units and finding areas and perimeters.

Directions for teachers:

1. Reproduce worksheets for students. Allow them to classify and reorder the geometric figures and regions as indicated.
2. Review vocabulary with class.
3. Review formulas for the areas of squares, rectangles, and triangles as needed.

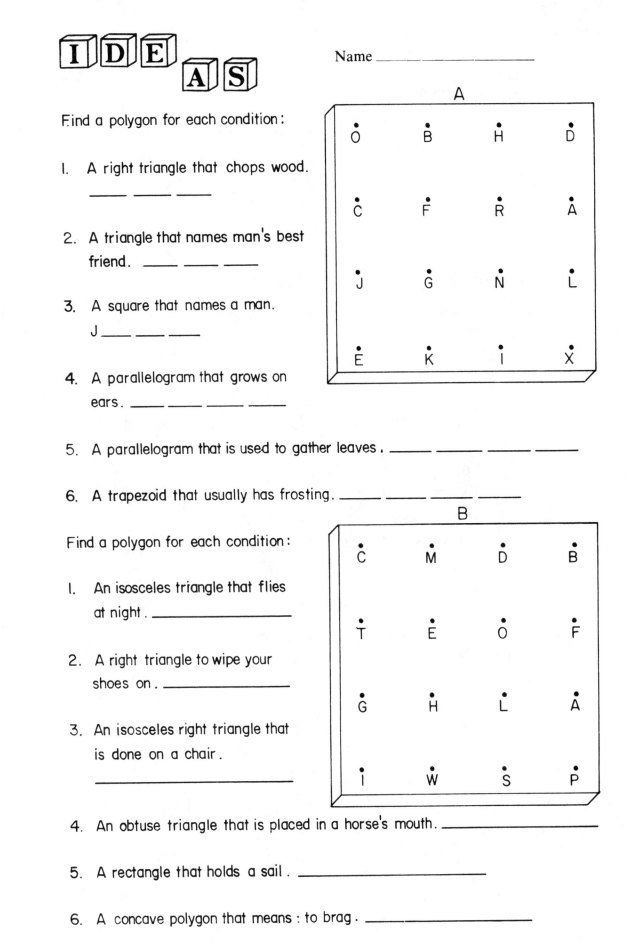

IDEAS

Name _____

A

O	B	H	D
C	F	R	A
J	G	N	L
E	K	I	X

Find a polygon for each condition:

1. A right triangle that chops wood.
   ____ ____ ____

2. A triangle that names man's best friend. ____ ____ ____

3. A square that names a man.
   J ____ ____ ____

4. A parallelogram that grows on ears. ____ ____ ____ ____

5. A parallelogram that is used to gather leaves. ____ ____ ____ ____

6. A trapezoid that usually has frosting. ____ ____ ____ ____

B

C	M	D	B
T	E	O	F
G	H	L	A
I	W	S	P

Find a polygon for each condition:

1. An isosceles triangle that flies at night. _____

2. A right triangle to wipe your shoes on. _____

3. An isosceles right triangle that is done on a chair.

   _____

4. An obtuse triangle that is placed in a horse's mouth. _____

5. A rectangle that holds a sail. _____

6. A concave polygon that means : to brag. _____

For Teachers

Objectives: Experience in visualizing special polygons

Directions for teachers:

1. Remove the activity sheet and reproduce a copy for each student.

2. Encourage students to visualize the polygons without actually drawing them.

3. Annouce that a key will be posted at a specific time.

4. Polygons are lettered clockwise or counterclockwise.
   (Normally BAND is not considered a polygon.)

Comments: Hand out 4-by-4 dot arrays that do not have letters. Challenge your language oriented students to make up similar sets of questions.

Key:
    A: 1. AXE 2. DOG 3. JOHN 4. CORN
              5. RAKE   6. CAKE
    B: 1. BAT 2. MAT 3. SIT 4. BIT
              5. MAST   6. BOAST

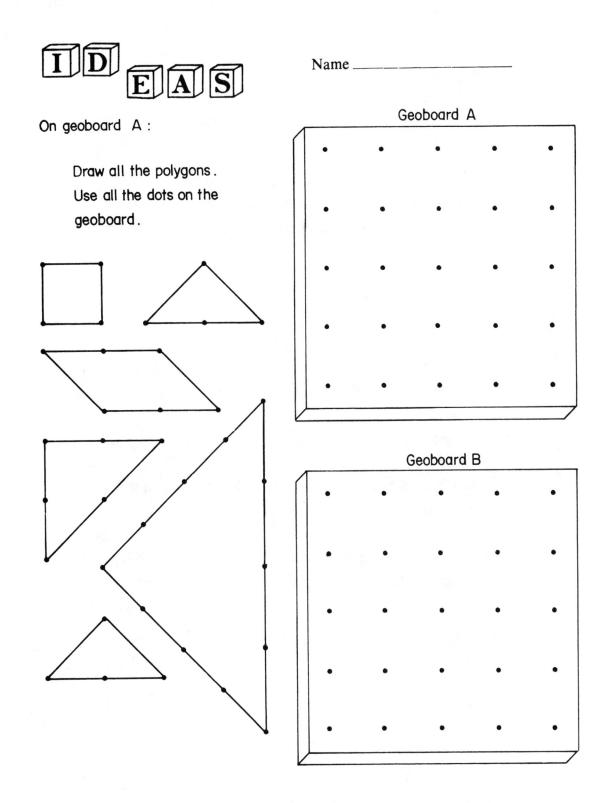

On geoboard A :

Draw all the polygons.
Use all the dots on the
geoboard.

Name _____

Geoboard A

Geoboard B

On geoboard B:

a) Draw one of the above polygons twice to form a right triangle.

b) Draw one of the polygons twice to form a square.

c) Draw one of the polygons twice to form a parallelogram.

 For Teachers

Objectives: Experience in visualizing and drawing composite polygons that requires a concept of congruence.

Directions for teachers:

1. Remove the activity sheet and reproduce a copy for each student.
2. Be sure each student has a straight edge but do not require that he use it.
3. Present this activity as a challenge. Don't expect a high level of success.
4. Announce that all correct solutions will be posted at the end of one week.

Comments: These experiences are similar to but considerably more challenging than their counterpart using tangrams. You may wish to extend this idea into the study of different shapes with the same area.

Key:

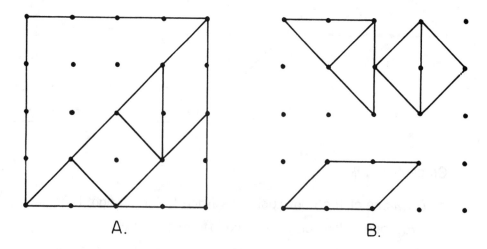

A.   B.

Name _____

3¢   5¢   7¢

How much are these?

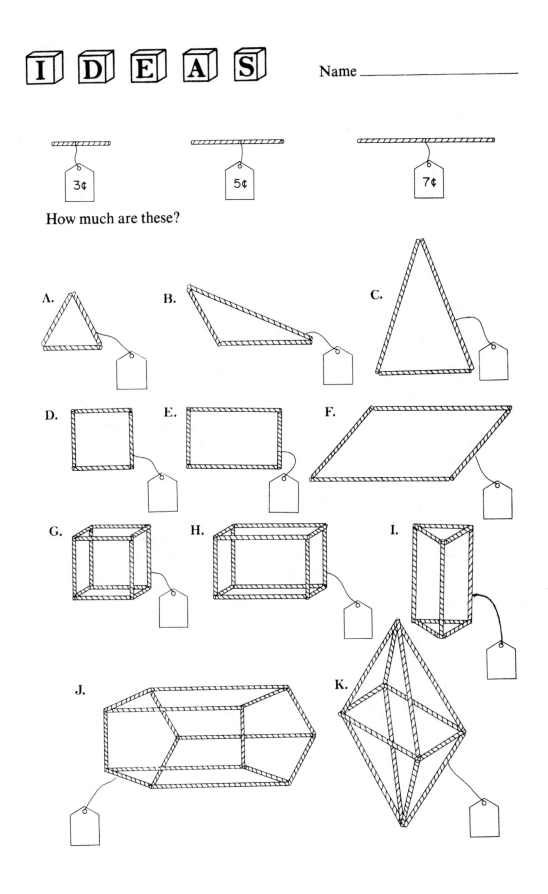

A.

B.

C.

D.

E.

F.

G.

H.

I.

J.

K.

⬜I ⬜D ⬜E ⬜A ⬜S For Teachers

Objective: Experiences with perimeter of polygons and identification of the edges of a solid

Directions for teachers:

1. Remove the student worksheet and reproduce one copy for each student.

2. After handing out the worksheet, ask the students to fill out the price tags on each figure.

3. When the students have completed their answers, discuss the different ways the students arrived at the answers: How did you know which straws make up the sides? Did you need to measure? Which polygons have the largest perimeters? What other polygons can you make from these straws? Can you make a polygon selling for 21 cents? For 13 cents? For 28 cents? What are possible prices for polygons made from these straws?

Comments: Students confuse the perimeter concept and the area concept because they don't have enough experience where the distinction is functional. There are few places in a student's life where he uses perimeter and area. An occasional contact in a classroom helps keep the distinction in mind. In many classes it would be appropriate to discuss the classification of triangles as equilateral, isosceles, or scalene. An investigation of pyramids, prisms, and other solids might also result.

Third and fourth graders would benefit by building some of the models, using straws and tape.

Answers

A. 9 B. 15 C. 19 D. 12 E. 16 F. 24 G. 36 H. 44 I. 33 J. 65 K. 72

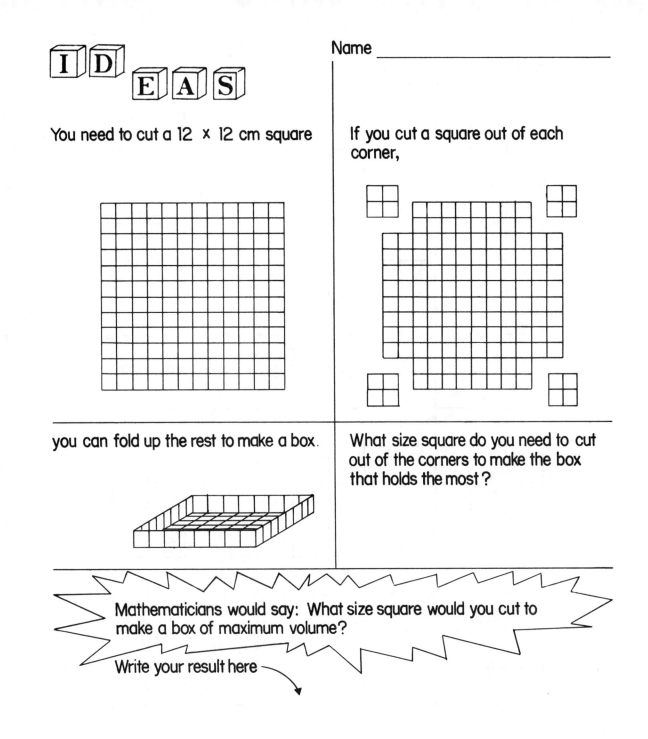

You need to cut a 12 × 12 cm square

If you cut a square out of each corner,

you can fold up the rest to make a box.

What size square do you need to cut out of the corners to make the box that holds the most?

Mathematicians would say: What size square would you cut to make a box of maximum volume?

Write your result here

Name _____

Situation: Sugar cubes have been stacked to form a cube. The outside of the large cube has been colored with red food coloring.

1. How many sugar cubes were used?_____

2. How many sugar cubes are painted

   a. on four sides?_____

   b. on three sides?_____

   c. on two sides?_____

   d. on one side?_____

   e. on *zero* sides?_____

3. Imagine you stacked 64 sugar cubes in the same way and painted the outside. Answer questions 2a through 2e for this cube and write your answers below.

   a. _____ b. _____ c. _____ d. _____ e. _____

4. Can you stack 1,000,000 sugar cubes on the teacher's desk? Explain your answer.

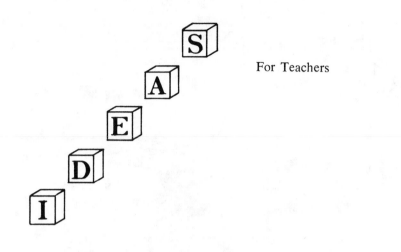

For Teachers

Objective: Experience in visualization of three dimensions

Directions for teachers:

1. Remove the student worksheet and reproduce one copy for each student. (Option) Display single copy on bulletin board.

2. Provide a box of sugar cubes and food coloring to model the picture.

Directions for students:

1. Study the situation and answer the questions.

2. When you finish question 3, I want someone to make a model of a "64" cube for the class.

3. Question 4 is a tough one you can work on.

Comments: The questions asked about the pictured "27" cube are appropriate for everyone in your class. Few students will be able to answer the same questions for a "64" cube unless they either build a model or make a drawing of a 4-by-4-by-4 cube. A drawing can be made quite easily by tracing the cube shown and extending the edges as shown:

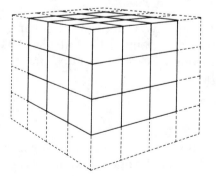

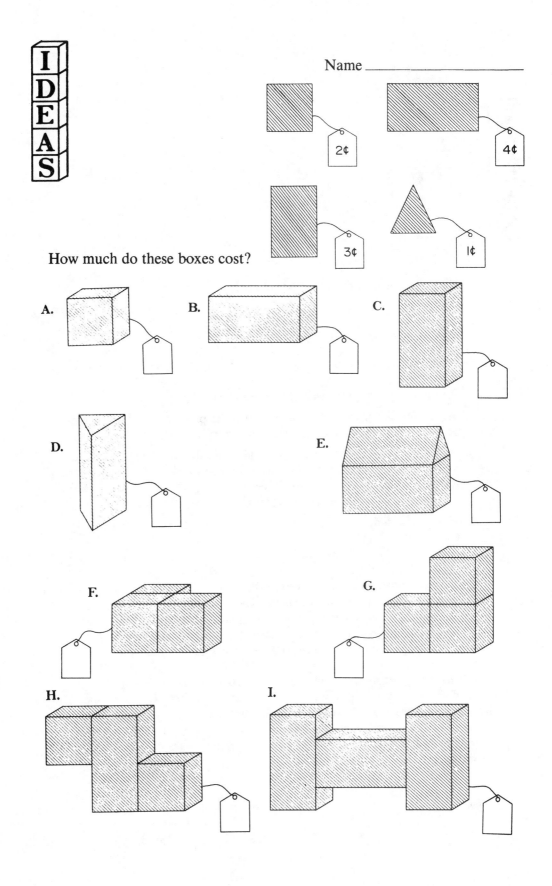

2¢

4¢

3¢

1¢

How much do these boxes cost?

A.

B.

C.

D.

E.

F.

G.

H.

I.

For Teachers

Objective: Experience with surface area of prisms

Directions for teachers:

1. Reproduce a copy of the worksheet for each student.

2. Hand out the copies and call attention to the prices of the four regions at the top of the page. Have the students figure out the price of each box.

3. When the students have completed the sheet, discuss their methods of arriving at the answers. Pay particular attention to F and G, which are different views of the same box. There are at least two possible answers for I, depending on whether the student "cuts" the 2¢ pieces.

4. Have your students design other boxes that could be constructed from these pieces.

Comments: Since the student lives in a three-dimensional world, he needs experiences in three-dimensional geometry. These activities provide experience in visualization. To answer the questions, he is forced to visualize the "back side" and to see the congruent pieces that make up the box. Boxes H and I are real challenges both to visualize and to keep track of the pieces that are used.

Expect that most students will figure each box one surface at a time; however, don't be surprised if a student notes that the cost of E can be found by combining the costs of boxes B and D and subtracting 8¢.

Even though your students won't have had instruction in perspective drawing, some will be amazingly adept at representing boxes they've designed themselves.

Answers

A. 12   B. 20   C. 16   D. 14   E. 26   F. 28   G. 28   H. 36   I. 56 or 52

Name _____

FACE OFF

This is one face of a
three-dimensional object:

Which of these objects have a
face to match it and, how many?

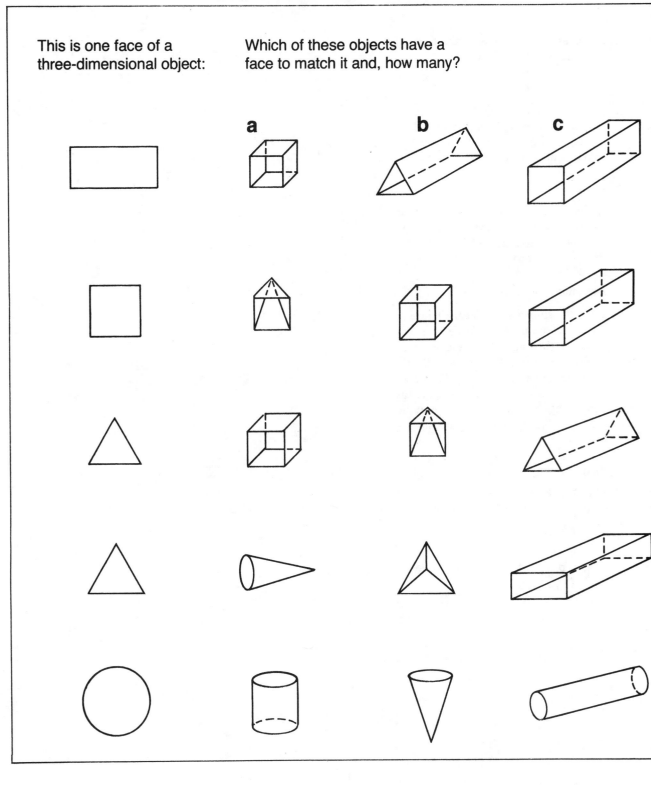

IDEAS

FACE OFF

Objective

To identify the shapes of the faces of three-dimensional objects.

Materials needed

Worksheet and pencils
Optional, but recommended: models of a cube, prisms, pyramids, a cone, a sphere, and a cylinder

Review

Be sure students know the names of the various three-dimensional figures and their characteristics, and how to identify the faces of these figures.

Directions for teachers

Have the students look at the figure in the left column and find the figure or figures to the right of it that have a face or faces the same shape. They should mark each correct answer; there may be more than one in a figure. Some students may find it helpful to use the concrete objects (models) to do this activity.

Answers

1. b, 3; c, 4
2. a, 1; b, 6; c, 2
3. b, 4; c, 2
4. b, 4
5. a, 2; b, 1; c, 2.

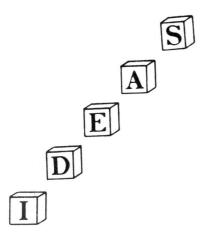

Use your conversion tables to help you complete this sheet.

PERSONAL DATA SHEET

Name: _____ Date: _____

Age: _____ years _____ months

1. Height: _____ feet _____ inches

   _____ centimeters

   _____ meters

2. Weight: _____ pounds

   _____ kilograms

   _____ grams

3. Waist: _____ inches _____ centimeters

4. Chest: _____ inches _____ centimeters

5. Span: _____ inches; _____ centimeters

6. Reach: _____ inches; _____ centimeters

7. Pace: _____ inches; _____ centimeters

8. Length of shoe: _____ inches; _____ centimeters

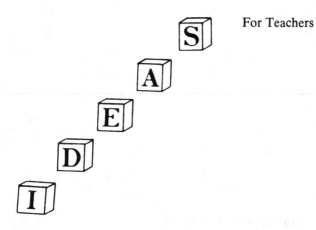

For Teachers

Objective: Experience in using conversion tables: English system to metric system

Directions for teachers:

1. Reproduce for each student a copy of the Personal Data Sheet and of the conversion tables on the inside back cover.

2. Place these pages on the activity table along with a tape measure, several rulers, and a bathroom scale.

3. Encourage students to fill out their Personal Data Sheet as an individual project. Allow a week for this "extra."

Comments: Some students may be sensitive about making "public" some of their personal data. You may avoid unpleasantness by allowing students to skip any data they consider too personal. Sorry, it is impossible to provide answers for the Personal Data Sheet.

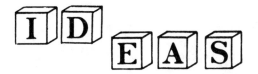

BODY RATIOS

Compare your body measures.

Record like this. ⟶
    Foot to height = 1 : 6

Around wrist to height = _____

Around wrist to waist   = _____

Around head to height   = _____

Around fist to waist = _____

Around wrist to neck = _____

Around neck to arm = _____

Arm to height = _____

Around fist to foot = _____

Foot to arm = _____

Around neck to height = _____

Compare your ratios with a friend's ratios.

 For Teachers

Objective: Investigating ratios using body measures.

Directions for teachers:

1. Remove the activity sheet BODY RATIOS and reproduce one copy for each student.

2. Give each student a piece of string. Make sure it doesn't have any stretch and is longer than he or she is tall.

3. Explain a way to record ratio. Use the poster HOW MANY FEET TALL ARE YOU? as an example. For example,

Foot:height   1 : 6

4. After all have finished, have the students compare similarities and differences.

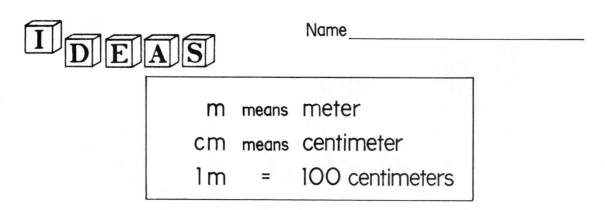

m	means	meter
cm	means	centimeter
1 m	=	100 centimeters

Circle the best measurement for each object pictured below.

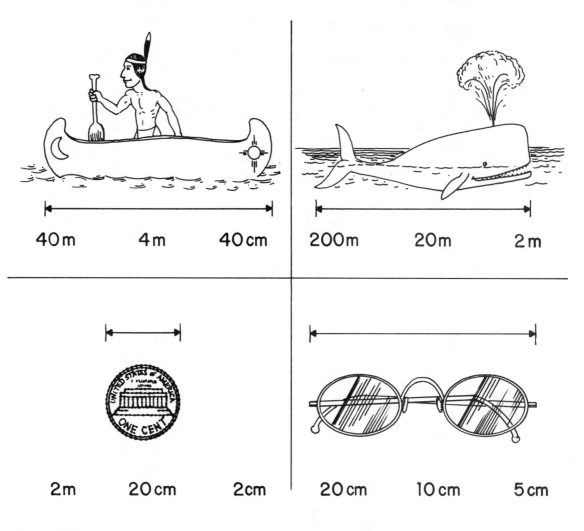

40 m	4 m	40 cm

200 m	20 m	2 m

2 m	20 cm	2 cm

20 cm	10 cm	5 cm

Circle the measurement in each pair that represents the shorter length.

4 cm, 40 m   8 m, 800 cm

7000 cm, 7 m   10 m, 100 cm

 For Teachers

Objective: To estimate measurements and to use the relationship between meter and centimeter

Directions for teachers:

1. The students need to have some experience measuring in centimeters and meters before they can be successful with the exercises.

2. Give each student a copy of the worksheet.

3. Students should imagine the actual objects pictured. The best measurement may not be exactly correct, so students should choose the one which is closest.

Ask students to explain how they decided which measurement is best.

4. Ask students to make up exercises like those on the worksheet.

Answers: canoe, 4 m; whale, 20 m; penny, 2 cm; glasses, 10 cm;
4 cm, 8 m = 800 cm, 7 m, 100 cm.

Comments: There are several ways to obtain answers to the exercises at the bottom of the page. In the first pair, 4 is less than 40 and cm is a smaller unit than m, so 4 cm is smaller than 40 m. Alternatively change one of the measurements in each pair to the unit of the other measurement; for example, since 7 m = 700 cm and 7000 cm = 70 m, the pair 7000 cm, 7 m is the same as the pair 7000 cm, 700 cm or the pair 70 m, 7 m.

IDEAS

Sizing Up The Situation

Circle the best answer.

1. If an elevator can hold ten average eighth graders, is its weight limit 8 kg, 80 kg, 800 kg?

2. You could probably eat 10 g, 500 g, 1000 g of pancakes and drink 10 mL, 500 mL, 1000 mL of juice for breakfast.

3. If you filled your empty car tank with gas, you would put in 8 L, 80 L, 800 L.

4. If a bridge has a weight limit of 5 metric tons, then 2 cars, 10 cars, 20 cars could use it at one time. (Note: The symbol for metric ton is t and 1 t = 1000 kg.)

5. You probably weigh about 4 kg, 40 kg, 400 kg.

6. An individual-sized carton of milk holds about 2 mL, 25 mL, 250 mL.

7. Your books for three classes together weigh approximately 3 kg, 30 kg, 300 kg.

Try this experiment:

Find and record the weights (masses) of one liter of water, juice (or some other liquid), rice, sand, and dried beans. Be sure to weigh the container when it is empty and subtract its weight from the total.

1 L of	water,	juice,	rice,	sand,	beans,
weighs	_____ g;	_____ g;	_____ g;	_____ g;	_____ g.

---

8. Based on the results of the experiment, does one milliliter of water weigh 1 g, 10 g, 100 g?

Discuss your answers to the questions with your classmates. Be ready to prove that your answers are correct.

SIZING UP THE SITUATION

For Teachers

Objective

Experience in estimating the weight and capacity of everyday objects and experimenting with the relationship between liters and grams.

Materials needed

• Scales or balances with weights to measure in grams; a scale that measures a person's weight; liter container; containers calibrated in milliliters; and one liter of water, juice, rice, sand, and dried beans.

Review

Be sure students understand that capacities are measured in liters (L) and milliliters (mL), and that weight (mass) is measured in grams (g) and kilograms (kg).

Directions for teachers

Distribute the worksheets. Have the students circle the best answer for each of the multiple-choice questions. They should also do the experiment. Discuss the answers for all questions and have students prove their answers to classmates in case of a question.

Answers

(1) 800; (2) 500, 500; (3) 80; (4) 2; (5) 40; (6) 250; (7) 3; (8) 1.

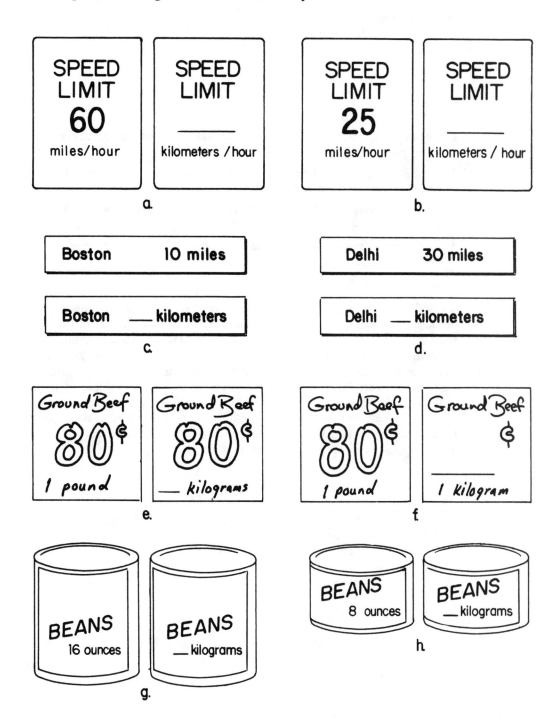

Complete the signs for the metric system.

SPEED LIMIT 60 miles/hour

SPEED LIMIT ____ kilometers / hour

a.

SPEED LIMIT 25 miles/hour

SPEED LIMIT ____ kilometers / hour

b.

| Boston | 10 miles |

| Boston ____ kilometers |

c.

| Delhi | 30 miles |

| Delhi ____ kilometers |

d.

Ground Beef **80¢** 1 pound

Ground Beef **80¢** ____ kilograms

e.

Ground Beef **80¢** 1 pound

Ground Beef ____ ¢ ____ 1 kilogram

f.

BEANS 16 ounces

BEANS ____ kilograms

g.

BEANS 8 ounces

BEANS ____ kilograms

h.

Objective: Experience in using conversion tables:
English system to metric system

Directions for teachers:

1. Reproduce for each student a copy of the activity sheet and the conversion tables printed on the inside back cover.

2. Have students work independently or in groups of two. Encourage them to find the easy way by using the tables.

3. Post the answers to **a** and **b** in one location so that students may check their work before proceeding.

4. Post the remaining answers in a second location. Have students check their own papers.

Comments: The apparent inconsistencies in the tables due to rounding to the nearest hundredth should be discussed, especially with the more capable students. For example, note that though 6 centimeters is 3 times 2 centimeters, the corresponding table entry—2.36 inches—is not precisely 3 times .79 inches. This "rounding problem" may bring up an interesting discussion regarding which is the more defensible answer for exercise **a**—96.6 kilometers an hour or 96.60 kilometers an hour? Of course the answer is neither! People just don't make speed limits to that degree of precision. The most likely equivalent speed limit would be 95 kilometers an hour, or possibly 100 kilometers an hour. Thus the answers given below are somewhat ambiguous.

Answers

a. 95 (96.6)   **b.** 40 (40.25)   **c.** 16 (16.1)   **d.** 48 (48.3)   **e.** .45
f. $1.76   **g.** .45   **h.** .225